Antonia Till, freelance editor, researcher, publisher's reader and sporadically dedicated cook, lives in London with her family and cats.

Loaves

— & —

Wishes

Writers Writing on Food

EDITED BY ANTONIA TILL

Published by Virago Press Limited 1992
20–23 Mandela Street, Camden Town, London NW1 0HQ

Reprinted 1992

A CIP catalogue record for this book is available from the British Library

Printed in Great Britain

ACKNOWLEDGEMENTS

Permission to reproduce texts from the following books is gratefully acknowledged: 'Bread' from *Murder in the Dark* by Margaret Atwood. Jonathan Cape, 1984 and Phoebe Larmor; *Nursery Cooking* by Molly Keane, Macdonald, 1985; *The Golden Notebook* by Doris Lessing, Michael Joseph, 1962; Maxine Hong Kingston for 'Dishwashing'.

The photographs of Margaret Drabble, Germaine Greer, Attia Hosain, Rana Kabbani, Kathy Lette, Sara Maitland, Susie Orbach and Marina Warner are by Charles Hopkinson. The photograph of Margaret Atwood is by Graeme Gibson, Maeve Binchy by Liam White, Shashi Deshpande by Ramaa Tirumalachar, Molly Keane by Dermot Donohue, Maxine Hong Kingston by Franco Salmoiraghi, Elean Thomas by Humphrey Nemar and Virginia Woolf from Hulton Picture Library; 'Robyn Archer (Lederhosen and Fatsuit) sings Schönberg and eats an apple at the same time. The Seymour Group production of *Pierrot Lunaire*, Sydney 1990, directed by Barry Kosky, designed by Michael Anderson' is by Robert Macfarlane.

Every effort has been made to trace copyright holders in all copyright material in this book. The editor regrets if there has been any oversight and suggests the publisher is contacted in any such event.

If you plan for a year, plant a seed. If you plan for ten years, plant a tree. If for a hundred years, teach the people. When you sow a seed once you reap a single harvest. When you teach the people you reap a hundred harvests.

K'uan-Tzu (551–479 BC)

CONTENTS

INTRODUCTION

It is a measure of the extraordinary esteem in which Oxfam is held world-wide that writers from Tokyo to London, San Francisco to Bangalore, Jamaica to Sydney, Dublin to Delhi, have responded with such alacrity and generosity to our request to write for this anthology. Interestingly, not one of the many people who have made the project possible has questioned the decorum of writing about food as a way of celebrating and supporting Oxfam's fiftieth anniversary. Indeed, more than most of us, the dedicated workers for Oxfam, at headquarters or in the field, are daily faced with the centrality of food in human society. It is in the Afterword that Robert Cornford of Oxfam tells us something about the work and aims of Oxfam, and of the global questions raised by the issue of poverty.

Of the themes which have emerged – in such diverse voices – a powerful one is the way food is so often an affirmation of humanity, of civility and sociability. Germaine Greer, in her piece on famine, points out that '[e]specially if we are a peasant people, we are what we eat', and tells of the true charity with which a poor Ethiopian community shared their sparse supply of millet-based staple food, *n'jera*, with a convoy of famine-stricken refugees, and how the victims' faces 'lit up with real joy'. It is this humanity which, provided we are above the barest subsistence and not subject to the famine which means grubbing for roots or eating our seed corn, seems to require that our meals, however exiguous, are accorded the dignity of careful preparation, the grace of sharing. Shashi Deshpande remembers a woman who lived with her family on the streets of Bombay: 'I saw them ... at their dinner as I passed by. "Want to join us?" she asked me, with a smile as bright as the fire on which I had seen her cooking earlier.' Writers of the prosperous North, even those for whom cooking is an oppressive chore or a source of self-doubting anxiety, acknowledge that a meal shared by friends and family is one of the bonding rituals without which the family, society even, can fall apart. Benoîte Groult, with Gallic vigour, asserts that 'true conviviality can only flourish during a good meal, lovingly prepared ... that good food and wine quicken the intelligence, mellow the mood and stimulate conversation'.

For food is, delightfully, an area of licensed sensuality, of physical delight which will, with luck and enduring tastebuds, last our life long. Taste, texture, sensuous combinations, do not have to be conjured with expensive ingredients. The smell of newly-baked bread is almost a cliché for whole-some pleasure; the eggplant or aubergine dip for which Rana Kabbani gives us the recipe is, even in countries where the vegetable has to be imported, a far from extravagant dish. Yet its tenderly verdant smokiness is Lucullan in its luxury.

Robyn Archer's travelling woman has a song of joyous remembrance:

Three-course dinner on the terrace
overlooking Lipari
Pasta fresca, marinara
insalata mista, Oscar, painter's wife, and twins and me

Chinatsu Nakayama charmingly celebrates the different noises appropriate for eating various sorts of noodle in Japan, a respectful and subtle discrimination to be accorded to one of the most universal Japanese foods. And Marina Warner, in her devilish short story, wittily embodies the fragrant seductiveness of exotic fruit.

It is in rejecting simple, wholesome sensuousness, the healthy respect for food which requires in some societies that 'not a piece of bread can be thrown away without kissing it and raising it to one's eyes as with all things holy' (Attia Hosain), that we in the prosperous North insult the famished children, women and men of the impoverished South. Susie Orbach demonstrates the grotesque dislocation of a society where women, surroun-ded by superfluous plenty, starve themselves, occasionally even to death, in the pursuit of some oppressively imposed ideal of appearance and feminin-ity, while their sisters in the South may be involuntarily, desperately, starving.

Even in the rejection of food there is often a power-play. Anyone who provides food learns that the spurning of food they have provided is often disproportionately wounding, and may discover in themselves, if they are very honest, the power they wield through the act of providing. This power may well be manipulative, as Maeve Binchy demonstrates with warm comedy in her short story. And sometimes it is the only kind of power women are permitted to employ. Even for liberated women the kitchen can be a place of power as well as of warmth and nurturing, and is often, unofficially, her office and administrative centre. Recently, exiled from my house for nearly six months, I came to realize that the main reason for my feelings of rootlessness and disenfranchisement was my lack of a kitchen. My family benefited from the flurry of exuberant cookery which marked my reinstatement.

Nevertheless, we should not forget that the kitchen area of a yacht is, with facetious accuracy, nicknamed the 'galley'. The majority of the world's women are, all too literally, galley-slaves. Even the women of the North, dowered with machines, gadgets and choice, are burdened with the necessity of providing food for their families, day after day, week after week, year after year. As Benoîte Groult points out, any failure to do this with a good grace is readily equated with a failure of love. Shashi Deshpande writes of the 'angry orchestra women beat out on pots and pans'. Sara Maitland is uncompromising: 'I hate to cook'. She reflects on the joy she experienced while breastfeeding her children, but loathes, resents, rails against the daily chore of planning, and usually executing, meals. Margaret Drabble confesses, 'Food and the preparation of food have been the source of some of the most powerful anxieties of my life'.

Throughout the world it is the women who bear the responsibility for feeding their families. In countries devastated by drought and deforestation it is the women – and sometimes the children – who spend up to seven hours a day just gathering the firewood or water. And that is before the picking, cleaning, sorting, grinding, pounding, preparing and cooking such ingredients as they can obtain.

What you will find in this anthology is a variety of responses to the request to write something, anything, about food. You will discover anger, wit, fantasy, storytelling, joy, poetry, autobiography and argument. And it amounts, gloriously, to a celebration, of food, of variety, of resourcefulness, of love and, above all, a desire to help Oxfam.

My gratitude to the writers who have made this anthology is almost beyond expression. Each of them is distinguished, each is busy with her own work and the many calls on her time which are consequent on that distinction, yet all have been magnanimously ready to contribute to this collection. Thank you, all of you, for the generosity of your response and the extraordinary quality of your writing. I am enormously grateful to Charles Hopkinson, the talented and busy photographer, who made time in his frantic schedule to take the superb photographs of those writers who were to be found in the UK. Many thanks are due too to Robert Cornford of Oxfam for the sustained enthusiasm he brought to this project, and to Mary Davis, who made me welcome at the Oxfam headquarters and provided the information for the food facts which intersperse the contributions. And thank you, my colleagues at Virago, especially Lennie Goodings and Karen Cooper, for the patient and affectionate support you have given me throughout.

You too, the reader, thank you for acquiring this book and for your implicit support of the work of Oxfam. Attia Hosain writes, 'My wise old Ayah used to say "An empty stomach cries out for an answer".' Today that cry is loud in the world.

Antonia Till

MAEVE BINCHY

Maeve Binchy is Irish, born in Dublin, and graduated from University College Dublin. At first a teacher and travel writer, she has written plays for theatre and television as well as her bestselling novels and short stories. She lives in Dublin.

Listen to Mother...

MAEVE BINCHY

BELLA's mother knew everything. She knew how to read palms, she could sing calypsos, she could revive tired dead flowers, she remembered people's birthdays, she worked in a fashion boutique where they said they would be lost without her because Bella's mother knew what would sell and what would not.

The only thing she hadn't known was that her daughter Bella would not be beautiful.

'Do you think I could be called Arabella?' Bella had asked when she was seven, a square, stocky girl with round glasses.

'Nonsense, that's not your name.'

'But they said at school that Bella meant beautiful, and everyone laughed.'

'They won't always laugh. Listen to Mother. The day will come when you will be very beautiful, very beautiful indeed.' Bella believed her, everything that Mother said would happen did happen. After all Mother had promised that they would move from the damp flat in the shabby house where they lived when Father left. She had told Bella not to cry. She must listen to Mother, and smile like a happy little five-year-old, everything would be all right. And shortly after that they went to live with Uncle Charlie in a bungalow. Uncle Charlie wasn't there all the time, he had another home somewhere that Bella wasn't to ask him about. But she was to be very nice to him at meals and everything would work out fine.

Uncle Charlie said that Mother was the best cook in the world. It's the way to a man's heart, well, one of the ways, he would say, and laugh at Mother in a knowing sort of way that Bella never understood.

Mother always set the table well. She had four tablecloths and matching napkins; they didn't need any ironing and were pink and yellow and green and white, a different one each day, and always a flower to go with them. The flowerseller said Bella's mother was a real lady, and used to give her one daffodil, or a single rose. Uncle Charlie used to say that it was a pleasure to put his legs under Mother's table and indeed anywhere else. Other women were careless, they didn't know how to make a man feel welcome.

And the food. Mother never served the same thing twice. Home smelled of fresh coffee, homemade bread, there were always a couple of fresh oranges in the white china bowl in the kitchen. Uncle Charlie said it was like heaven on earth, after a lifetime of package juice and shop bread and cheap instant coffee.

'I like to make things nice for you, Charlie. You're so good to us,' Mother said over and over.

Bella knew that her mother bought shop brown bread and warmed it up, that she added a little orange zest to the package orange juice. That the coffee was instant but a coffee bean always roasted on the stove to give the right aroma. But Bella had always been asked to listen to Mother, not to explain Mother to Uncle Charlie.

They left Uncle Charlie when Bella was nine and went to live with Uncle Adam. Uncle Adam had just bought a big terraced house and Mother said it would be a wonderful opportunity to live in a truly gracious home at last. Mother was going to decorate it because Uncle Adam was busy and would be away a lot.

'Does he have a second home like Uncle Charlie?' Bella had been sad to leave the bungalow and Uncle Charlie's winks and jokes, which she had never understood but had seemed good natured.

'Listen to Mother, and don't talk about Uncle Charlie or any nonsense about other homes. Just smile and be nice to people and do your homework, you'll have a lovely bedsitting room all of your own in this house. Do you understand me, darling?' Bella had sort of understood, and Uncle Adam was very very nice too. And he loved Mother's cooking.

Uncle Adam cared about his health. He was a fitness fanatic and Mother seemed to know exactly what was delicious and yet good for him. He marvelled at the way she could produce dishes that were almost fat-free, that were low in cholesterol. The woman was a genius, he said over and over again. And the silent smiling Bella, who always went to her bedsitting room immediately after she had cleared the table and loaded the dishwasher, agreed. Her mother was a genius. Bella had seen a lot of butter and cream going into the dishes that were meant to be made with low-fat yoghurt and fromage fraîche. And by now she knew very well that life was much easier if you did listen to Mother rather than challenging her.

Mother seemed to be delivering too on her promise of making Bella beautiful. Uncle Adam paid for contact lenses as a fifteenth birthday present,

4

and Mother arranged a 900-calorie diet which meant she lost her puppy fat. Mother's boutique always had clothes that suited Bella going very cheaply. Mother got her a good hairdresser and by the time Bella left school nobody thought it in any way unusual that her name should mean beautiful. In fact several of the boys had said it was very apt indeed.

Bella wished she could be like Mother and accept their compliments. She really didn't begin to know the language of flirtation and it was no use listening to and watching Mother in this, because it seemed to change from hour to hour, whatever the occasion demanded. And it changed from man to man. Uncle Adam left to take up a job abroad, a job that involved taking his wife with him.

Mother cooked him a wonderful dinner the night before he left, with shining crystal and flickering candlelight.

Uncle Adam seemed to be very apologetic about going, but Mother was a fount of understanding, and bravery and encouragement.

'You're the most amazing woman I ever met,' he said. There was truth in his eyes. Bella wanted to cry.

Mother just smiled, a great warm forgiving smile.

'Not a word of recrimination,' he said.

Bella wondered why there should be any recriminations. Mother had got this magnificent house and everything in it. Mother would forget Uncle Adam.

Mother's next friend was not called Uncle, he was called Mike. He was ten years younger than Mother and ten years older than Bella. He was very handsome, he was a singer. Mother went to gigs on the back of his motorbike, Mother made wonderful suppers for his friends. The silver and the good cut-glass were always put away. Locked away, actually, when the friends arrived with their leather jackets.

Mother served huge pots of chilli or trays of lasagne; young people liked the freedom to invite half a dozen others along, they much preferred that to things being perfect. You had to judge each situation by its own merits.

Bella did a secretarial course. She studied hard and, even though Mother hadn't asked her to, she stayed away from home a lot. It often seemed to her that Mike and his friends were more her age, and she knew Mother wouldn't like that. If Mother noticed she said nothing, but she was even more warm and supportive than ever. She coached her for the job interviews and wasn't in the least surprised when Bella got a job as secretary and researcher to a well-known Professor at the University.

'Invite him to dinner, darling,' Mother said. 'He's a widower, he has terrible terrible college food, or opens tins of beans, he'll be a walkover if you cook him something half-way good. He'll be putty in your hands.'

'I don't want him to be putty in my hands, I just want to work for him,' cried Bella.

Mother was planning: 'I'll keep Mike out of sight. Listen to Mother, Bella, this is a classy house, he'll know you come from something if he sees you here in this setting.'

'I don't WANT to seduce him!'

'Well, darling, don't you think you should think of seducing someone? You are nineteen, after all. At your age . . .'

'I don't want to hear, please, Mother.'

'You haven't done badly by hearing and listening to me.' Mother was huffy now.

'But I don't want to do some fake feast for this man . . . don't you understand?'

Mother didn't understand, she truly didn't. There was no question of a fake feast. Serving a man a good meal was what a woman did. Men went to war, men ran governments, controlled the City, decided how things would be. With a few token exceptions that's the way it had always been and would always be. Listen and believe, Bella.

Bella wished she had asked her mother all those years ago to make her intelligent, not beautiful. Mother was so clever she might well have done it, rather than letting Bella languish in the B stream, missing A-levels, not stirring her mind to think independently and forcefully. She would love to have answered Mother, because she knew that there must be an answer.

Mother's moods never lasted long.

'If not this man, then some other man, Bella. I'll show you how to cook your way to his heart. It's what life is all about.'

Bella worked for her Professor, a kindly man more interested in Elizabethan musical instruments than the present day. Sometimes Bella looked at him and wondered whether her mother would have been able to entrap him to live with her and support her through some cunning cookery. It was quite possible. Uncle Charlie and Uncle Adam had been unlikely starters, and who could have been less likely than Mike? Bella felt a wave of grudging admiration for her battling mother with the bright restless eyes, who thought that nothing was impossible.

'What are you thinking about? You're smiling,' the Professor asked her.

'Oddly enough, I was thinking about my mother,' she said.

'Good thoughts?'

'Yes mainly. She's like Auntie Mame a bit.' Her laugh was infectious.

'Lucky you, mine was like Mrs Danvers in *Rebecca*.' He laughed too.

He asked her out. To the theatre. To the opera, to the cinema, to the theatre again.

'No dinner?' Mother asked.

'No, Mother, and PLEASE don't set up a meal plan for me. I couldn't bear it.' Her eyes filled with tears of panic.

'A little after-theatre supper, the two of you by the fire here, crusty bread, a really good soup with aïoli . . .' Mother's eyes had lit up.

Bella knew the time had come to stop Listening to Mother. She told the Professor. She spoke to him in a way that Mother would never have talked to Uncle Charlie, Uncle Adam, Mike or indeed Mr Harrison, who looked very like someone who was going to replace Mike.

She told him as they walked together through the University campus. About how food was used as seduction, as a silken cord to bind. Bella's face was flushed and excited as she assured her Professor that she could never do anything like that, work out in advance what tastes, aromas and presentation would enslave him. It wasn't that she didn't love food, she did, but it had to be fair.

He took her face in both his hands and kissed her.

'I suppose she'll be spaced out, organizing the wedding breakfast now,' he said.

'Mother doesn't go in much for weddings,' Bella admitted.

'We don't have to listen to her on that one either,' he said.

Irish Stew
2 lb best lamb
1 lb potatoes
1 lb onions
chopped mint and thyme
three cups of water
seasoned flour

The meat must be really good quality, cut into thick chunks. Coat it with the seasoned flour, then alternate layers of sliced potatoes, sliced onions and cubed lamb until the saucepan or casserole dish with its tight-fitting lid is full. Sprinkle the thyme and mint at intervals as you are building up the layers and make sure you end up with a layer of sliced potatoes on the top.

You add the water, and the secret is to use this small amount because you want the potatoes to turn into a mush with the meat juices.

Sometimes people add a handful of barley to the mixture, but the purists think that you shouldn't put in carrots or other vegetables.

Cook either on the top of the stove or in the oven for around two hours. The aim is to have the potatoes at the bottom of the dish dissolve and absorb the meat juices.

The thing to avoid is having the whole thing swimming in watery liquid.

EDITOR'S NOTE

Irish Stew is a traditional one-pot dish, the proportions of which can vary according to numbers and the state of household finances – from the comparatively lavish version given here to mostly vegetables, just flavoured with meat.

GERMAINE GREER

Germaine Greer is Australian. After convent schooling and graduating in Australia she came to Britain. Renowned as a feminist writer and scholar, she is also a courageous and curious traveller, and a skilled and original gardener. She lives near Cambridge.

Famine

GERMAINE GREER

'IF they're that hungry,' said the man from the American relief organization, 'they'll eat anything.' He was wrong, of course. Hunger is the best sauce only until it turns into starvation. Starving people are not hungry. Starving people have no appetite at all. Hunger is healthy; most of us need to feel it far more often than we do. Starvation is sickness in mind and body. Pathogens that the healthy body kept at bay overwhelm the starving body, while terrible grief and shame set up their camp in the soul. The worst insult that you can fling at a peasant is to call him 'starveling'; '*morto di fame*' is still in rural Italy a term of the deepest contempt. To be dying of hunger is to have failed everything and everyone; to watch the people you love growing more ghastly and skeletal day by day is mental torture of the most exquisite.

I had asked the aid official why the people of Wollo were expected to eat their pancakes without salt. The pancakes were made of wheat flour, 'Gift of the EEC to the People of Ethiopia', according to the sacks. (As there was a dire shortage of sacks those words appeared on much more food than the EEC ever sent, but no one accused us of making false claims.) Even if the people of Wollo had grown wheat, they would be hard pressed to make something edible of nothing but wheat. In fact, they often just roasted wheat kernels, and very good they were. But the flour had to be made into something, something that weak, sick, dispirited people could manage to chew and swallow. The result was a pancake; try it sometime. Try mixing flour and water and roasting it in a hot pan. The Ethiopians who manned the communal kitchens, for there was too little fuel wood for people to do their own cooking, even supposing they were strong enough to carry firewood and water, did their best; but the pancakes were hard and leathery. People died with segments of uneaten pancake in their carrying cloths. I bethought me of our butter mountain which could so easily have been turned into a *ghee* lake. And I remembered a famine relief effort of a very different kind in Salt Lake City, behind Calcutta, in 1972.

The Indian government relief effort was different because, first of all, it was in time. Nine million people were helped before they became unable to help themselves. And the relief effort was run by people as poor as the refugees, who knew what was important to them. At Salt Lake I was amazed to see that people were issued, not just with their sack of wholewheat flour (much more useful than the bleached and refined stuff we would have given them), but a small onion, a cardamom and a clove. A row of makeshift booths had grown up along the main concourse, and there the people bartered the day's spice for a different spice, for a spoonful of turmeric or a few grains of black pepper, instead. The fare was frugal, but they could vary it, so that it had the scent of home.

The stuff that was cooked up in the communal kitchens at Bati was what Australians call damper, a flat bread made of flour-and-water dough and roasted in the open fire. Aborigines now mix the dough with a can of Foster's and a very large quantity of baking soda. White bushmen salt it, but aborigines are – or used to be – unique among the world's populations in that they do – or did – not use salt. The original of damper, the aborigines' flat bread called *ntara*, was not made out of flour, but of all kinds of seeds, especially grass seeds, ground between two stones. The nomads did not carry the stones, which lived in the places where the seeds grew, to be used by all who passed by. The 'Afghans' (who were really Pathans) who brought their camels to central Australia, soon learnt how to find the stones and how to incorporate the local grains in their *chapatis*, which is why they thrived in the deserts where the white man died of hunger. It is a great irony of history, that if Australia had been settled by Asians instead of Caucasians, the landscape would not have been destroyed by hard-hoofed animals and rabbits and *ntara* would still figure on the world menu.

If Australians ate *ntara*, the Ethiopians might not have had to gag on their EEC flour pancake. On my third visit to Ethiopia in 1985 I saw famine victims given the food they love, which they call by a name strangely like the aborigine name for damper, *n'jera*. I was travelling with a busload of settlers down from Wollo to Asosa; as many of the people, having never ridden in a motor vehicle, were travel-sick, the buses did not travel overnight. Paramedics checked each passenger, pulling aside ragged cloaks and peering into wizened faces. The sick, who protested loudly, terrified that the convoy would go on without them, were taken to special tents and bedded down on deep straw. Over the hill came the good matrons of the town, their immaculate white cottons billowing around them. Each one carried a plastic bucket, and in each bucket trembled fold upon fold of grey spongy *n'jera*. The people smelt it before they saw it. When the tin plates were put in their hands and they saw the wobbling folds with their own eyes, their faces lit up with real joy. And they ate. They ate as I had never seen anyone in a famine shelter eat. They were a people transformed. They were themselves again. Especially if we are a peasant people, we are what we eat.

The people of that town had made a sacrifice, for the *n'jera* they made for the settlers was all *t'eff*; elsewhere people were eating half and half. *Eragrostis t'eff* is cultivated only in the Ethiopian highlands; the harvest that fails year after year because of exhaustion of the soil is the *t'eff* harvest. Only the Dutch, to my knowledge, have made any attempt to grow *t'eff* in order to provide the Ethiopians with new seed stocks. If we grew *t'eff* we would quickly undersell and outproduce the Ethiopian farmers, so that our attempt to make up their shortfall would eventually ruin them. Unless. Unless we became connoisseurs of *n'jera* and paid as much money for the real thing as we are happy to pay for a wine grown (from American grapes) in a certain part of France. Unless Ethiopian cooking became one of the great cuisines of the world.

One of the best meals I ever had in my life was the simplest Ethiopian meal of all, *n'jera wat*, the *n'jera* of Lent. If good cooking is a question of proportion and balance of scent and texture, that meal of *n'jera* with a spicy lentil stew and a raw tomato was perfection. I had grander meals in Ethiopia. I was once hand-fed in the traditional Ethiopian fashion by a gold-encrusted colonel in the Ethiopian army, who tore off pieces from a square yard of *n'jera*, packed them with choice morsels of meat marinaded in *birberi* and poked them into my mouth, which was forced to gape so wide to accommodate them that I felt like a fledgling. The dishes were brought to the table by a succession of the most beautiful young soldiers that ever wore uniform. But I remember more vividly the small café where the waiter brought a bucket of water and soap so that patrons could wash in the yard, where the patrons prayed before they ate, and where a perfect meal cost me sixpence.

SHASHI DESHPANDE

Shashi Deshpande is Indian, a novelist who also writes short stories and children's books. Graduating in both Economics and Law, she has also studied English literature. She lives in Bangalore.

Of Kitchens and Goddesses

SHASHI DESHPANDE

IT was a large kitchen, spacious enough to contain two cooking areas. One of these was for boiling the milk, making the tea and for all the cooking that wasn't part of the main meal of the day. This, the lunch, was cooked in a corner which was sacrosanct – only those women who did the cooking could go near it. They sat in a sort of shallow pit, cooking on two pairs of baked-mud stoves in an arched recess which housed the chimney. Close at hand, a niche in the wall held the essentials – salt in a jar, the oil can and the spices box, wooden, dark and grimy with age. What intrigued me most were the slings hanging from the rafters, swinging lazily when touched, their strings darkened to the colour of the soot-darkened walls, in which were stored little vessels. What was in them? Anything, I imagined, that had to be kept out of the way of the cat which lay indolently near the threshold, unaware, it seemed, of the temptations overhead. Nevertheless, one sensed a canny look in its eyes, a kind of concealed energy in the furry body, that made you feel it was only biding its time, waiting for the right moment to rouse itself and make a mighty spring upwards. 'Shoo, shoo', each woman hissed as she daintily side-stepped the cat. The soft muted miaows it made in reply are part of the sounds of that kitchen for me, blending with the monotonous drone of women talking, the hollow sound as they blew at the fire, the thwack as they knocked two pieces of wood together to make the fire burn brighter. It seemed such a safe secure world – the vision of a child who stood outside the threshold and looked into that world.

I stopped being a child, I grew up, I got married and had a kitchen of my own. Yet it seems to me I continued to stand outside. Until the day my mother-in-law, showing me her calloused hardened palms, said, neither complaint nor self-pity in her tone, 'I used to make fifty to sixty *bhakris* [a flat, dry bread] every morning. Sometimes,' she went on, 'I think I was born only for this.' Coming from a prosaic, matter-of-fact woman who never spoke of 'Life', nor indeed of any generalities, it was an astonishing statement. Perhaps it was at that moment that I stepped over the threshold and into the kitchen. For, as if the focus had shifted, my vision suddenly changed. And, instead of that safe warm haven of my childhood, I saw another kitchen, where the women were chained to endless, tedious labour, crouching for hours before a smoking fire. Accompanying this picture were no pleasant sounds, but the angry orchestra women beat out on pots and pans.

I have a small statue of a goddess with me, a goddess who holds a ladle as large as herself in both her hands. She is Annapurna, the goddess of bounty, given to brides on their wedding day. Marking out their roles for them. Henceforth you are Annapurna, the provider. But to place the statue among your gods and to worship her was not enough to make you an Annapurna. There was a long hard way to be gone through before you could reach the pedestal. The cooking, as I remember it, was immensely complicated, with endless restrictions and infinite imperatives. Apart from the daily routine cooking, there were always festivals, death days, weddings and ceremonies – each of which called for a different set of dishes. The kitchen was the testing ground where a woman proved herself. It was almost literally an ordeal by fire. Can you make *ghee* [clarified butter] the right shade of brown and grainy enough? Have your *chapaties* [soft, flat bread] the right number of layers and are they satisfactorily light? Can you cook an entire meal if guests unexpectedly turn up in the middle of the night? Can you serve properly, the right things in the right place and the right quantity for each person?

And there were the rules, the rigidity that allowed no options, gave no room for skimping, for taking an easy way out. Leftovers were unclean and therefore fresh meals had to be cooked each time. Meals were at unearthly hours on the day after an *Ekadashi* [the eleventh day of a lunar fortnight] or when there was an eclipse. There was no day on which someone wasn't fasting. Almost always it was the women who fasted, though this never exempted them from cooking an entire meal for those who weren't fasting. And even after you had proved yourself worthy with this back-breaking endless work, the very meals you had cooked could be turned into a weapon against you. To see a man push away his plate in anger, the food uneaten, and walk away was an awesome, a terrifying sight. The women cowered in guilt, overcome by an immense sense of wrongdoing, even if the man's anger had nothing to do with them.

There's a story about the saint Meerabai, whose enemies once sent her a snake concealed in a basket of flowers. In spite of knowing what was inside, she opened the basket and fearlessly put the snake around her neck. And behold! It was transformed into a garland of fragrant flowers. So you turn a weapon into an expression of love. Transform it into a means of pleasure. I've seen women, who are supposed never to eat until everyone has been fed, sit down to a late meal, all the food in their midst, a hodgepodge of plates before them, weary, but with a sense of great ease about them. Conversation flows, so does laughter. Food is relished, discussed and enjoyed and the women politely squabble over the last bits left. The hard work of *papad* [poppadum] or pickle-making, or the drudgery of the preparations before a wedding, became a convivial social gathering. Women gossiped and match-made, they laughed and joked as they rolled and pounded, while little girls earnestly carried the wet circles of *papads* and arranged them in the sun to dry, ready to turn them over the instant they began to curl. And on fasting days, endless variations could be rung on the few permissible items, resulting in such delicious food that as children we clamoured to join the fasting women, instead of eating the dull everyday routine meal of rice-*dal-chapaties*-vegetables.

Did these women ever say in an apologetic, self-deprecatory tone, 'I'm only a housewife' or 'I only cook'? I never heard these phrases from that generation. On the contrary, they had an enormous pride in their skills. 'Your aunt is a good cook,' my uncle said to me (and how dull, how flat the phrase 'good cook' seems when I think of the infinite resonances of the Marathi word that was used instead!), and my aunt proudly accepted it as her due. Women wore the praise like a medal, a badge of honour. Skills became legends in families. 'Nobody can make pickles like my mother used to.' 'When my grandmother made *mandgis* the whole village used to come and watch.' An aunt who was trying to explain, through an interpreter, the method of making *chirotés* to an Englishwoman who had married into the family, interrupted her to repeat, 'Tell her the syrup must be two-strings; remember, two-strings,' she emphasized. The Englishwoman nodded; but thinking of what syrup-making was like for me – an endless dipping of fingers into the fiery blob of sugar to test, resulting in blistered fingertips, but rarely the correct 'two-string' consistency – I wondered whether she understood what it really meant. For my mother, for my aunt, there was never any hesitation. Only a certainty. It is ready. And it was. The *chirotés*, multi-layered and crisp, dipped into it, came out succulently golden and sweet.

'You can't hurry cooking,' my mother-in-law used to say as she let the *dal* simmer for hours in a stony jar on a tiny fire, the spices permeating the liquid while it simmered, finally becoming a harmony of tastes and smells. 'You have to put your heart into it,' a friend's mother told us when we admired her *modaks*, the shape as perfect as the *gopuram* [cupola] of a temple, the taste ambrosial, the bland softness of the rice-flour covering a perfect foil for the fragrant cloying sweetness of the jaggery-coconut-cardamom filling. I remember once asking my mother for the recipe of a *pulao* that was a proud family tradition – a three-layered, three-coloured rice dish with spicy fried balls of *khoya* [milk solidified by prolonged cooking] concealed within. My aunt, who had been listening while my mother told me the ingredients, disagreed violently about one of the spices mentioned. There was an impassioned argument between the two of them and later, each of them came to me and told me to be sure and do it her way, with such feeling that to do it either way would be to betray the other.

I have never done it. Labour an entire day for one dish? From the very beginning, something in me resisted that sticky shining trap they set for women with the bait of being a goddess. And the story doesn't end there. Just to be a provider is never enough. You have to be something more – or is it something less?

> 'If you serve milk and rice to everyone/ and content yourself with plain rice alone/ we shall be able to say you are the proper/ daughter of a wise father.'

I read these words of a Bengali folksong and wondered – when and where along the way did she become a goddess of self-denial? 'Anything will do for me.' 'I'm not really hungry.' 'If you are all satisfied, I am too. I don't need to eat.' The movies have now institutionalized this martyred woman, the mother with her constant self-deprivation and saintly smile. Whenever I'm driven into a frenzy by her, I like to think of another woman, who sold medicinal herbs and roots on the pavement near my home in Bombay. That bit of the pavement was her home. A trunk held her belongings, her baby was slung in a hammock tied to the palings, an older child played about, and, when he was not working, her husband sat by. In the evenings she 'closed shop' and cooked the family meal. I saw them, the whole family, the woman too, at their dinner as I passed by. 'Want to join us?' she asked me, with a smile as bright as the fire on which I had seen her cooking earlier. I often think of that smile. It denied martyrdom, it rejected self-sacrifice. The woman was alive – not just surviving, but alive.

The other day, when shopping, I heard a young couple argue about buying a loaf of bread. 'It's a waste to buy the large loaf,' the girl said. 'But some of the guys said they might be dropping in,' the man replied. 'I don't want any guys dropping in today,' she muttered. Is Annapurna tottering? But there's a friend who showed me the kitchen in her new home with the words, 'This is my office.' I knew what she meant. This is where I do the work I want to, the work I like and enjoy.

20

No, Annapurna still stands firm. No longer on the pedestal, perhaps, but on the ground. And maybe, she can now lay down her ladle whenever she gets tired. After all, being a goddess can be very tiring.

The Bengali folksong quoted above (translated by Lila Ray) has been taken from *Women writing in India – 600 B.C. to the Present*, ed. Susie Tharu and K. Lalita, published in India by Oxford University Press.

Khichdi and Kadhi

Here is the recipe for one of the simplest and humblest of Indian dishes. I chose this, not only because I wanted to avoid anything extravagant or complicated, but also because the khichdi, combined with kadhi, is a meal in itself and a dish that is eaten, with some variation, perhaps, in a great number of regions in India.

Ingredients for the *khichdi*

one cup rice
moong dal, a variety of lentils (half the quantity of the rice)
1 tbs cooking oil, mustard seeds and turmeric for seasoning
Powder together four to six cardamoms, six or eight cloves, two or three pieces of cinnamon and a teaspoonful of cumin seeds

Roast the *moong dal* to a light brown, and wash it along with the rice. Mix salt and the powdered spices with this and let it stay for a while. Heat the oil and add mustard seeds. As soon as they stop spluttering add the turmeric powder. Pour in the rice-*dal* mixture, roast it for a minute or two, then add sufficient water. Let it cook slowly on a low fire.

Ingredients for the *kadhi*

two cups of sour curds
1 tbs *gram* flour [*besan*]
a half-inch piece of fresh ginger
1 tsp of cumin seeds
two or three cloves
a few fenugreek seeds
oil
pinch of asafoetida and turmeric powders and some curry leaves

Beat the sour curds very gently, adding the flour of *gram dal* [*besan*] to thicken it. Grind together cumin seeds, ginger, cloves and fenugreek seeds (with green chillies for those who don't mind them). Heat 1 tsp of oil, add mustard seeds. When they stop spluttering, add the asafoetida and turmeric powders. Take off the heat and add a few curry leaves. Pour this on the sour curds. Put it on the fire, and keep stirring continuously; when it reaches the boiling point and becomes a frothy, creamy homogeneous mixture, take it off the fire. Add salt and ½ tsp sugar. Garnish with coriander leaves.

This is eaten with *papads*, pickles and maybe a salad.

EDITOR'S NOTE

In these quantities, with the addition of papads *(poppadums) and pickles (see page 51), this dish is ample for four. The spices should be obtainable in sizeable towns, and are much cheaper in Asian shops than in the little jars sold by supermarkets. Asafoetida needs to be stored tightly sealed, as it gives off an odd smell until cooked. Strained natural yoghurt can be used for the curds. The* moong dal *can be roasted either by being swirled in a heavy frying pan (skillet) over medium high heat or spread out on a baking tray in the oven. Two green chillies give a flavour which is probably quite fiery enough for Western palates. The hands should be washed very thoroughly after handling them, as chilli juice can sting the skin and hurt the eyes.*

Maxine Hong Kingston is American, but her books, both fiction and non-fiction, explore the myths, tradition and history of her Chinese ancestors. She lives in Oakland, California.

Dishwashing

MAXINE HONG KINGSTON

DISHWASHING is not interesting, either to do or to think about. Thinking has dignified other mundane things, though. At least it will postpone the dishwashing, which stupefies. After eating, I look at the dishes in the sink and on the counters, the cat's dirty bowl and saucer underfoot, swipe at the dabs and smears recognizable from several meals ago, pick up a cup from among the many on chairs and beside beds, and think about suicide. Also about what to write in the suicide note.

The note is an act of kindness. The criminals who most upset us are the ones who refuse to give satisfying motives. 'I don't want to wash the dishes one more time.' A plain note, no hidden meanings.

I run water into the frying pan – its black underside just clears the faucet because of the pile-up – but the scrubber and the sponges are hidden somewhere in the bottom of the sink. Thwarted at the start. The frying pan fills; the pile shifts; greasy water splashes on me and spills. I turn off the water and get out of the kitchen. Let the pan soak itself clean. No way to wash the pot and the blender underneath it nor the dishes under that, the crystal wine glasses at the bottom. The dishpan and the drain are buried, too, so I can't let the cold, dirty water out. When the mood to do so overcomes me, I'll take these dishes out and start all over.

Once in a while, early in the morning, my powers at their strongest, I can enjoy washing dishes. First, reorganize the pile, then fill the dishpan again with clean water. I like running water on my wrists and the way bubbles separate from the suds and float about for quite a while. I am the one who touches each thing, each utensil and each plate and bowl; I wipe every surface. I like putting the like items together back on the shelves. Until the next time somebody eats, I open the drawers and cupboards every few minutes to look at the neatness I've wrought.

Unfortunately, such well-being comes so rarely, and the mornings are so short, they ought not to be wasted on dishes. Better to do dishes in the afternoon, 'the devil's time', Tennessee Williams calls it, or in the evening immediately before dinner. The same solution for bedmaking – that is, right before going to bed. I try to limit the number of items I wash to only those needed for dinner, but since I can't find them without doing those on top, the obstructing ones get washed too. I trudge. I drudge.

The one person I know who is a worse dishwasher than I am pushes the dishes from the previous meal to the middle of the table to make places for clean saucers, no plates left.

Another person pulls a dish out of the sink and uses it as is.

When my father was a young man, working in a laundry on Mott Street in New York, he and his partners raced at meals. Last one to finish eating washed the dishes. They ate fast.

Technology is not the answer. I have had electric dishwashers, and they make little difference. The electric dishwasher does not clear the table, collect the cups from upstairs and downstairs, scrape, wipe the counters and the top of the stove. One's life has to be in an orderly phase to load and arrange the dishes inside the dishwasher. Once they're gathered in one spot like that, the momentum to do the rest of the task is fired up.

Although dishwashing is lonely work, I do not welcome assistance. With somebody else in the kitchen, I hurry to get at the worst messes to spare her or him. Alone, I wash two plates, and take a break. Helpers think that dishwashing includes unloading the dishwasher, sweeping and mopping the floor, defrosting the refrigerator, and de-crusting the oven, cleaning the kitchen, and cleaning the dining room.

In *Living Poor With Style*, Ernest Callenbach says that it is unsanitary to wipe dry because the dishcloth spreads the germs evenly over everything. Air drying is better, he says, meaning letting everything sit in the drainer. (He also recommends washing the cooking implements as you finish each step of cooking. Impossible. I did that once in a temporary state of grace, which was spoiled by having to wash dishes.)

Paper plates are no solution. There are no paper pots and pans and spatulas and mixing bowls. The plates are the easiest part of dishwashing.

I prop books and magazines behind the faucet handles. Some people have television sets in their kitchens. Books with small print are best; you don't turn the pages so often and dislodge the book into the water.

I do enjoy washing other people's dishes. I like the different dishes, different sink, different view out the window. Perhaps neighbours could move over one house each night and do one another's dishes. You usually do other folks' dishes at a holiday or a party.

I like using a new sponge or dishcloth or soap or gloves, but the next time, they're not new.

In *Hawaii Over the Rainbow*, Kazuo Miyamoto says that in the World War II relocation camps for Americans of Japanese ancestry, the women had the holiday of their lives – no cooking, no dishwashing. They felt more at leisure than back home because of the communal dining halls and camp kitchens. I can believe it.

Compared to dishes, scrubbing the toilets is not bad, a fast job. Also you can neglect toilets one more week, and you only have one or two of them.

I typed a zen koan on an index card, which I have glued to the wall beside the sink. You may cut this out and use it if you like:

> 'I have just entered the monastery. Please teach me.'
> 'Have you eaten your rice?'
> 'I have.'
> 'Then you had better wash your bowl.'
> At that moment, the new monk found enlightenment.

This koan hasn't helped yet with the dishwashing, and it would probably be more enlightening to cut out Miyamoto or Callenbach's words. But I have a glimmering that if I solve this koan, I can solve dishwashing too, or if I can solve dishwashing, I can solve life and suicide. I haven't solved it but have a few clues.

The koan does not say that the monk was enlightened after he washed the bowl. 'At that moment' seems to be at the moment that he heard the advice.

I hope the koan doesn't mean that one has to pay consequences for pleasure; you eat, therefore you wash bowl. Dismal. Dismal.

It could mean something about reaching enlightenment through the quotidian, which is dishwashing.

The monk did not gain his enlightenment after washing the dishes day after day, meal after meal. Just that one bowl. Just hearing about that one bowl.

I have come up with a revolutionary meaning: Each monk in that monastery washed his own bowl. The koan suggests a system for the division of labour. Each member of the family takes his or her dishes to the sink and does them. Pots and pans negotiable. Cat dishes negotiable too.

The koan shows that dishwashing is important. A life and death matter, to be dealt with three times a day.

VIRGINIA WOOLF

Virginia Woolf, one of the most admired and innovative British novelists of this century, was born in 1882. Her novels date from soon after her marriage to Leonard Woolf, and she was also a distinguished critic, journalist and essayist. Prone to appalling depressions, she drowned herself in 1942.

From: To the Lighthouse

VIRGINIA WOOLF

Now all the candles were lit, and the faces on both sides of the table were brought nearer by the candlelight, and composed, as they had not been in the twilight, into a party round a table, for the night was now shut off by panes of glass, which, far from giving any accurate view of the outside world, rippled it so strangely that here, inside the room, seemed to be order and dry land; there, outside, a reflection in which things wavered and vanished, waterily.

Some change at once went through them all, as if this had really happened, and they were all conscious of making a party together in a hollow, on an island; had their common cause against their fluidity out there. Mrs Ramsay, who had been uneasy, waiting for Paul and Minta to come in, and unable, she felt, to settle to things, now felt her uneasiness changed to expectation. For now they must come, and Lily Briscoe, trying to analyse the cause of the sudden exhilaration, compared it with that moment on the tennis lawn, when solidity suddenly vanished, and such vast spaces lay between them; and now the same effect was got by the many candles in the sparely furnished room, and the uncurtained windows, and the bright mask-like look of faces seen by candlelight. Some weight was taken off them; anything might happen, she felt. They must come now, Mrs Ramsay thought, looking at the door, and at that instant, Minta Doyle, Paul Rayley, and a maid carrying a great dish in her hands came in together. They were awfully late; they were horribly late, Minta said, as they found their way to different ends of the table.

'I lost my brooch – my grandmother's brooch,' said Minta with a sound of lamentation in her voice, and a suffusion in her large brown eyes, looking down, looking up, as she sat by Mr Ramsay, which roused his chivalry so that

31

he bantered her.

How could she be such a goose, he asked, as to scramble about the rocks in jewels?

She was by way of being terrified of him – he was so fearfully clever, and the first night when she had sat by him, and he talked about George Eliot, she had been really frightened, for she had left the third volume of *Middlemarch* in the train and she never knew what happened in the end; but afterwards she got on perfectly, and made herself out even more ignorant than she was, because he liked telling her she was a fool. And so tonight, directly he laughed at her, she was not frightened. Besides, she knew, directly she came into the room, that the miracle had happened; she wore her golden haze. Sometimes she had it; sometimes not. She never knew why it came or why it went, or if she had it until she came into the room and then she knew instantly by the way some man looked at her. Yes, tonight she had it, tremendously; she knew that by the way Mr Ramsay told her not to be a fool. She sat beside him, smiling.

It must have happened then, thought Mrs Ramsay; they are engaged. And for a moment she felt what she had never expected to feel again – jealousy. For he, her husband, felt it too – Minta's glow; he liked these girls, these golden-reddish girls, with something flying, something a little wild and harum-scarum about them, who didn't 'scrape their hair off', weren't, as he said about poor Lily Briscoe, 'skimpy'. There was some quality which she herself had not, some lustre, some richness, which attracted him, amused him, led him to make favourites of girls like Minta. They might cut his hair for him, plait him watch-chains, or interrupt him at his work, hailing him (she heard them), 'Come along, Mr Ramsay; it's our turn to beat them now,' and out he came to play tennis.

But indeed she was not jealous, only, now and then, when she made herself look in her glass, a little resentful that she had grown old, perhaps, by her own fault. (The bill for the greenhouse and all the rest of it.) She was grateful to them for laughing at him. ('How many pipes have you smoked today, Mr Ramsay?' and so on), till he seemed a young man; a man very attractive to women, not burdened, not weighed down with the greatness of his labours and the sorrows of the world and his fame or his failure, but again as she had first known him, gaunt but gallant; helping her out of a boat, she remembered, with delightful ways, like that (she looked at him, and he looked astonishingly young, teasing Minta). For herself – 'Put it down there,' she said, helping the Swiss girl to place gently before her the huge brown pot in which was the Boeuf en Daube – for her own part she liked her boobies. Paul must sit by her. She had kept a place for him. Really, she sometimes thought she liked the boobies best. They did not bother one with their dissertations. How much they missed, after all, these very clever men! How dried up they did become, to be sure. There was something, she thought as he sat down, very charming about Paul. His manners were delightful to her, and his sharp cut nose and his bright blue eyes. He was so considerate. Would he tell her – now that they were all talking again – what had happened?

'We went back to look for Minta's brooch,' he said, sitting down by her. 'We' – that was enough. She knew from the effort, the rise in his voice to surmount a difficult word that it was the first time he had said 'we'. 'We' did this, 'we' did that. They'll say that all their lives, she thought, and an exquisite scent of olives and oil and juice rose from the great brown dish as Marthe, with a little flourish, took the cover off. The cook had spent three days over that dish. And she must take great care, Mrs Ramsay thought, diving into the soft mass, to choose a specially tender piece for William Bankes. And she peered into the dish, with its shiny walls and its confusion of savoury brown and its bay leaves and its wine, and thought, This will celebrate the occasion – a curious sense rising in her, at once freakish and tender, of celebrating a festival, as if two emotions were called up in her, one profound – for what could be more serious than the love of man for woman, what more commanding, more impressive, bearing in its bosom the seeds of death; at the same time these lovers, these people entering into illusion glittering eyed, must be danced round with mockery, decorated with garlands.

'It is a triumph,' said Mr Bankes, laying his knife down for a moment. He had eaten attentively. It was tender. It was perfectly cooked. How did she manage these things in the depths of the country? he asked her. She was a wonderful woman. All his love, all his reverence had returned; and she knew it.

'It is a French recipe of my grandmother's,' said Mrs Ramsay, speaking with a ring of great pleasure in her voice. Of course it was French. What passes for cookery in England is an abomination (they agreed). It is putting cabbages in water. It is roasting meat till it is like leather. It is cutting off the delicious skins of vegetables. 'In which,' said Mr Bankes, 'all the virtue of the vegetable is contained.' And the waste, said Mrs Ramsay. A whole French family could live on what an English cook throws away. Spurred on by her sense that William's affection had come back to her, and that everything was all right again, and that her suspense was over, and that now she was free both to triumph and to mock, she laughed, she gesticulated, till Lily thought, How child-like, how absurd she was, sitting up there with all her beauty opened again in her, talking about the skins of vegetables. There was something frightening about her. She was irresistible.

CHINATSU NAKAYAMA

Chinatsu Nakayama is Japanese. She has been a member of a famous theatre group and has acted on television. After helping to found a women's liberation group she became involved in politics and is now a member of the Upper House. She lives in Tokyo.

Noodle Sounds

CHINATSU NAKAYAMA
Translated by ELIZABETH WOOD

OREIGNERS inevitably mention *sushi* when they discuss Japanese cuisine. But people especially familiar with Japanese culture may argue that *kaiseki ryori* – that meal composed of a multitude of tiny, elegant dishes – is the most Japanese of foods. What many people may not realize is that Japanese almost never eat homemade versions of either dish. Both are very difficult to make.

For *sushi*, you start out by cooking rice and adding a touch of flavouring with vinegar, sugar and salt; this provides the base used for *sushi*, known as *sushimeshi*. First the chilled *sushimeshi* is shaped in the palm of the hand into the well-known bite-sized rectangles, then a bit of grated horseradish is added, and finally a thin slice of raw fish or an entire, small shellfish is placed over all. This dish, eaten dipped into soy sauce, is called *nigiri*, which means to hold or grasp; the name comes from the action of patting the rice into shape. There are many different varieties of *sushi*, but the one known abroad is this *nigiri*.

Requirements for making *nigiri* include particularly good rice – cooked well – and many different kinds of fresh fish and seafood. While there's no reason why one couldn't just eat ten pieces of, say, tuna *nigiri*, for some reason it isn't done that way. We only really feel we've had *nigiri* if we've eaten ten morsels of ten different kinds of fish.

Naturally, it's not easy to prepare ten different kinds of fish at home. Also, fresh fish has recently become extremely expensive. *Nigiri* was invented and first offered for sale by some now-nameless entrepreneur back in early nineteenth-century Edo (present-day Tokyo); it met with wild success and became a regular fixture in Japan. But, from the start, it was a prepared food,

37

rather than a dish to be made at home.

Kaiseki ryori is an elegant, full-course Japanese dinner. A huge array of ingredients prepared in many different ways are served in tiny dishes, carried in a few at a time. Even the order of presentation is dictated by tradition. The dishes all call for soy sauce and *dashi* (a fish stock made with dried kelp), yet it's a lot of work to prepare the variety of other ingredients involved in this colourful, many-course meal and, like *sushi*, it is almost never prepared at home.

Well then, you may ask, what *do* the Japanese eat at home? I remember a few years ago some research firm taking a survey into what home cooking children liked best. The results were: their first choice was hamburger, and their second was curried rice!

Parents in Japan live pretty much for their kids, which can be a good or a bad thing, depending on how you look at it. But in any case if kids like something, it's going to be made pretty frequently at home. Hamburger and curried rice have several things in common. First of all, they're very easy to make. If you prepare them with care, they can take time, but most Japanese know how to budget time. Often, products need only to be heated or thawed; you buy them practically done. Second, with prices what they are now in Japan, both are far and away cheaper than steak, and have a lot more volume than a package of frozen fish.

As for breakfast, many families eat bread, and most housewives are likely to prefer it. It's easier than making rice for breakfast, and is considered more fashionable. After the war, bread was substituted for rice in the lunches served in schools all over Japan. When I was a child – more than thirty years ago now – neither children nor adults liked bread. Everyone thought of it as being closer to cake than to real food. But the Education Ministry said it was more nutritious, and better. Experts supported the ministry in this. They said we lost the war because we'd always eaten nothing but rice. If we ate bread, we'd become as attractive as Westerners, they said. If we didn't start eating a lot of bread, cheese and meat, we'd never become fashionable, they gave us to understand. So, although children and adults alike preferred rice to bread, they began to try hard to scorn rice and favour bread.

We know now that Japan, after losing the war, was forced to import wheat flour in huge amounts, and that we were just helping our government out. It's ironic that by the time Western vegetarians and ecologists had begun to discover the value of rice and tofu, we had become completely accustomed to bread, and bakeries had sprung up throughout the larger cities, while rice farmers in the country hovered near death.

That's how modern children came to like bread. And because it's simpler to prepare, most wives like to have it for breakfast, provided that their husbands, whose age may make them resistant to bread, don't insist otherwise.

Most husbands have lunch near their offices. *Soba, udon* and *ramen* shops are everywhere, and reverberate with the sounds *fuu-haa* and *so-zo-zo-zo*.

Yes, since I'm writing this for publication in England, I wanted to be sure to mention those sounds. I was watching a TV talk-show the other day, and heard an American guest talking about them. His impressions went something like this:

> Was I ever surprised, the first time I went to a *soba* shop. The old guy next to me was carrying on, *fuu-haa, fuu-haa*. I naturally assumed he was ill. But then another old geezer started making noises like *so-zo-zo-zo-zooo*. 'Oh, Lord, everybody in here's sick,' I thought.

This American was a likeable guy, and I had to laugh along with him. But noodle sounds are actually a sore point in relations between Japanese and Westerners.

Two of the popular forms of noodles, *soba* and *udon*, are native to Japan, while *ramen* originally came from China. All three may be served either hot or cold, but are always served in a flavourful broth. With hot noodles, we always blow on them first, producing the sound *fuu-haa*. The noodles don't actually cool off just from being blown on, but we always do it anyway. Then, whether they're served hot or cold, the way we eat any noodles is to catch a few strands with the chopsticks, bring those that stay on up to the mouth and put just the ends of the strands into the mouth. Then we remove the chopsticks, and use them to help move any dangling strands upward. All the while, the noodles are being sucked in, making the sound *zo-zo-zo-zo*. We make this sound not only when we eat noodles, but also when we eat any type of hot soup or drink green tea.

Chazuke, green tea over rice, is frequently eaten as a light meal. It consists simply of a liberal amount of green tea poured over a bowl of rice, but nearly all Japanese like to eat *chazuke* while snacking on lightly-pickled vegetables and things. I like it a lot, too. This can be eaten in only one way: by holding the bowl in one hand, placing your lips on the rim, and raking the contents into your mouth with the chopsticks, meanwhile sucking in the tea. Naturally this makes quite an impressive noise. In addition to the sound *zo-zo-zo-zo* there's the clatter – *kacha-kacha* – of chopsticks as they hit the ceramic bowl. The other day, I was watching an old film, *Bakushu* [*Early Summer*], directed by Ozu Yasujiro, and couldn't help noticing the racket the lovely heroine made as she ate this same *chazuke*. I've heard that Ozu is known even in the West. My first thought was: won't Westerners be bothered by the discrepancy between her gracefulness everywhere else and her complete lack of table manners?

But she's not a dual personality. In Japan, along with the tea ceremony and the art of flower arranging, we've had schools of table manners for centuries, and according to their dictates, the eating of any kind of soup requires the making of a sound (granted, the level of the sound required is quite a bit more delicate than that which has evolved in modern times). What were always considered signs of ill-breeding in Japan were such things as making too overpowering a noise, letting the teeth grate together audibly (*kucha-kucha*) in chewing, and talking during the meal. I use the past tense here because, ever since Western manners have gained general approval, a certain amount of talking during meals has been encouraged. Once people tried talking while they ate, they found that it was a lot more fun, and now everyone chatters amiably through meals. Spaghetti is a grey area, but there would be something bizarre, to our minds, in eating *soba* or *udon* without making a sound. Noise is optional with consommé, but we feel there is something crafty and therefore disgusting about drinking *miso* soup or green tea silently. If making noise ever came to be considered rude, we wouldn't be able to eat *chazuke*. But Westerners say that our slurping is so disgusting it makes them want to faint. I'd feel bad if they keeled over, so I'm careful not to make noise in front of Westerners, but 'cultural exchange' is certainly every bit as tough as it's cracked up to be.

So what are married women up to while their husbands are making the sound *zo-zo-zo-zo* over lunch? If they're also working, they're likely to eat near the office. The occasional woman may make herself a lunch in the morning, when she's making her husband's and children's. Women who stay at home tend to make do on leftovers. Women have become a lot tougher in recent years, but their home life hasn't changed substantially: many men still take pride in the fact that they have never once set foot in the kitchen. Towards evening, women at home start getting ready to go out, and those at work hurriedly finish up the day's tasks, and both head for supermarkets near their homes, where they will buy the evening's curried rice or hamburger.

Of course, these eating habits are to be expected in a big city like Tokyo where everyone considers him- or herself middle-class (nearly everyone in Japan, for that matter, considers themselves middle-class). There is regional variation even in this small country, and places like Okinawa, which was annexed not long ago, remain nearly distinct cultures.

Yet, thanks to Japan's furious economic growth and reckless development, most areas have, over the last twenty years or so, lost any individual flavour they might once have had. Every small town has its 'little Tokyo' clustered around the station, and its scaled-down version of Tokyo culture. So I believe that the eating habits described here are, to some degree, common to the entire country.

But I am afraid that I may have given the impression here that our eating habits are more or less uncomplicated.

Actually, they have become very elaborate. Towards the late 1970s the Japanese began to take a great interest in food. Unwholesome characters with pretensions to gourmet lifestyles appeared on the scene, and cookbooks on every conceivable national cuisine jostled together on bookstore shelves. There are still a great many programmes on TV every day introducing new foods and their manner of preparation, and it's nearly impossible to find a magazine which doesn't have similar articles. Japan, historically inclined to take things in from other countries, has had not only French, but also Chinese, Korean and Italian restaurants for a long time, but the gourmet boom has given new life to the taste for international cuisine, to the point where it has now made its way into the average household.

Some decades ago, we had simple eating habits. For breakfast, *miso* soup, rice and pickles. On extravagant days an egg dish or some dried fish might be added. One would open one's aluminium lunchbox at school or at work, and find, time and time again, the same meal of rice and some kind of salty dish. Dinner was usually either fish or vegetables, boiled or grilled. People very seldom ate chicken or pork. When my mother was a child, the average family ate *sukiyaki* [beef and vegetables cooked in soy sauce, sugar and fish broth] only about once a year. When I was a child, it was still very rare to have beef, and on days when we were to have pork for dinner we knew something was up. Families were generally satisfied to eat more or less the same things every day.

But nowadays the wife who can't make Chinese and various Western foods in addition to Japanese food isn't thought much of a wife. Our country's cuisine has taken on a rather indeterminate internationalism, with coffee and English tea rivalling green tea in popularity. As a result, the Japanese wife who strives to be thought worthy of the name is plagued by a concern not so immediate for women in other countries: namely, fear of running out of storage space for her pots and utensils. She needs to have, at the very least, one set for Japanese foods, and separate utensils for Chinese cooking. Naturally, you can't eat Western food with chopsticks, and it would be gauche to drink coffee or tea from the handle-less ceramics used for green tea.

Here she runs up against a political issue. In Japan, the prices of land and costs of rent alike are prohibitive, and living spaces are shockingly cramped. Even the most devoted wife is hampered by considerations of space in her pursuit of utensils. She's likely to have many more than one family can use, and yet feel a nagging sense of their insufficiency as she glances about the kitchen, which has been made smaller than ever with the addition of extra shelving . . .

It isn't really so strange to make slurping noises while eating *soba*. But the way the Japanese people have bloated up as their economy soared does seem strange. More Japanese are now embarrassed to have foreigners hear their *zo-zo-zo-zo*, but I can't help thinking there are other things we should be embarrassed about first.

Umeboshi

Umeboshi is one of the Japanese's favourite pickled foods. Until a few decades ago it was often made at home. It is marketed now, but my mother still makes it every year. Tart and salty, it has a marvellous smell. It may be eaten while drinking green tea, or with rice or *chazuke*. It is sometimes used in cooking. It stimulates the appetite and promotes regularity.

Ingredients

Plum berries: Along with the cherry, the plum is one of Japan's best-loved trees. Its beautiful flowers bloom between February and April. The tree also produces a lovely green berry, which ripens and turns yellow in about June. Berries just on the point of turning from green to yellow are best for *umeboshi*. These may be found in any Japanese department store or supermarket at that time of year.

Shiso leaves: *Shiso* is a plant which smells much like basil, and is often used in Japanese cooking. There are green and red varieties; the one used in *umeboshi* is the red. In addition to lending the plum berries a lovely smell and rich colour, it also has sterilizing properties which prevent mould and allow the *umeboshi* to be stored for long periods. You will need about 10% of the volume of berries.

Salt: 20% of the volume of berries, and 20% again of the amount of *shiso* leaves. This amount of salt, of course, allows the *umeboshi* to be stored for long periods.

To Make

Plunge about 4½ lb of plum berries into water and soak overnight, to remove any bitterness.

Place the berries in a large bamboo basket and drain away the water. Prepare a clean crock. Prepare a little under 1 lb of salt. Place a layer of berries in the crock, and sprinkle with salt. Add another layer of berries, and sprinkle with salt again. Repeat this process until all the berries have been salted, then pour any remaining salt on top. Place a jar (wood is best but glass will do) slightly smaller than the crock, upsidedown over the berries, to help them retain their shape. Place a weight of about ½ lb on top of the wooden jar. For this purpose, a book or a stone will do. Set aside for two weeks. After just a few days a liquid will begin to rise around the berries. This liquid is called plum brandy.

At about the end of the two-week period, supermarkets will begin to carry the red *shiso* leaves. Wash well and drain about ½ lb of these, and rub them lightly with about 1 oz of salt. Wring them, and rub them again with a further 1 oz of salt. This will turn them dark purple. Then rub two or three tsp of plum brandy into the leaves. This will turn them bright red. Place the leaves on the very top of the plum berries.

About two weeks later – when a period of continued fine weather is predicted (in Japan, usually between the end of July through the 8th of August) – take out just the plum berries and spread them out in a large bamboo basket. Leave them in the sun to dry for two to three days.

Uncurl the *shiso* leaves and return the berries to the crock, placing the *shiso* leaves on top so that they cover the berries completely. Place a piece of paper over the mouth of the crock and fasten it with a cord. The *umeboshi* is ready to be stored. After six months it will be ready to eat, but the longer it is left standing the more intense the taste will be.

EDITOR'S NOTE

This dish is almost certainly unreproduceable outside Japan. It seems to have a distant relationship both with the English sloe gin and the lemons salted in oil of Middle Eastern cookery. The adventurous might try a version with small yellow plums (mirabelles) or even damsons, with handfuls of basil.

SOHAILA ABDULALI

Sohaila Abdulali was educated in India and the United States. Apart from her fiction she has written much distinguished journalism. For some years she was director of the Boston Rape Crisis Centre, and now works in sleep research and for Oxfam, dividing her time between the US and India.

Protection You Can Trust

SOHAILA ABDULALI

Sriram picked his way disgustedly through the alley, holding his grandmother's shopping bag with one hand and hitching up his pants with the other. He glared at his grandmother's sweaty back. She had never allowed him his dignity. Here he was, on his last day in India, twenty one, about to fly to America to get his degree, and she was making him go to the market and carry her bag like some coolie.

His grandmother stopped before an old man selling tomatoes, cucumbers, mangoes and coriander leaves. The mangoes were overripe and a cloud of flies hovered over them. Their heady smell warred with the crisp green chutney fragrance of the coriander.

Sriram's grandmother said, 'How much for the tomatoes?'

'Eight *rupees* for a kilo; look how good they are.' The old man held one up for her to inspect.

'Eight *rupees*! Look at this tomato, old man!' She fished out a small one with a bruise and shook it in his face.

'Arre! You try to make me starve, old woman! Take it for seven *rupees* and fifty *paise*, then.'

'Only if you give me a little *kotmir* to put in my curry.'

Sriram's grandmother picked up a fistful of coriander and pushed it into her bag.

Sriram looked around, wishing she wouldn't fight with everyone. He walked impatiently ahead, bumped into a woman walking in the other direction, and stepped into the gutter in his confusion. The woman passed on and Sriram looked furiously at his shoe, which was covered with a piece of black banana peel and a smear of green cowdung. He shook his foot and shouted to his grandmother, who was engrossed in a fight with an onion-seller, 'Dadi-ma! Let us go home.'

But it wasn't until after his bag was filled to bursting with fruits and vegetables, his pockets with ginger, garlic and cloves, that he was allowed to go home and change his shoes.

The West, he told Dadi-ma on the way home, would not be so dirty and chaotic. Yes, yes, they are so clean there, she agreed, thinking about which spices she would grind to a paste for Sriram's last curry. Cumin, coriander, garlic, fenugreek and turmeric, and she would coat the fish with it.

When Sriram's plane took off at three-thirty the next morning, he drew a deep breath and smelled fish curry as he was borne upward. The plane hurtled toward the United States, and Sriram tossed fitfully among the clouds, dreaming visions of Dadi-ma weeping as she burned chillies to remove the evil eye from him, of his last visit to the incense-filled altar room to kneel before the gods and goddesses, of the acceptance letter from Harvard inside his suitcase, and of fish curry.

The kitchens in graduate housing were all the same: small, white and immaculate. On the wall were three hooks for pans and a laminated sign entitled 'Pest Control: Do's and don't's.' Sriram put his pile of books on the table, pushed aside *Managerial Finance, Free to Choose* and *Business Accounting* and opened *Quick Meals for the Single Person*. He had reached the stage of settling in when he had to fill the kitchen and bathroom closets. There was one store where he could get everything, his host family had said.

His host family lived on Beacon Hill and had a very nice house. Alan, who was big and blond, clapped Sriram painfully on the back every time they met, and said, 'So, what do you think of America, huh?'

Sriram, trying to wriggle his bony shoulders free of the giant pink hand clutching them, would smile tentatively and say, 'I like it. It's very clean, it's very efficient, it's very – civilized. Not like my country, everything is a mess, ha-ha.'

And Alan would clap him on the back again and say, 'Yeah, you sure are lucky you made it here.'

'You sure are lucky, you *sure* are lucky.' Sriram practised saying 'sure' with an American accent while he flipped through his cookbook and made a list of things to buy. When he was done with that, he stuffed the list into his pocket and went downstairs to walk to class.

It was drizzling grey-green rain needles as he walked through the yard. He walked with his book bag over his head to keep his hair dry. Then he noticed that no one else was doing that. The other people in the Yard either had raincoats or umbrellas, or were simply getting wet and holding their bags at their sides. In confusion, Sriram lowered his bag and held it awkwardly by his side, letting the cool rain nuzzle down his neck and down the back of his new Harvard sweatshirt. And since no one else was running through the puddles to class he didn't run either, but walked sedately and damply on.

At Xavier's College in Bombay, he thought, everyone would have been using whatever they could grab to keep dry, and carrying their shoes in their hands as they walked through puddles.

In class, he looked around and saw that no one took off their shoes, and so his stayed on as well, although in a few minutes his toes curled uncomfortably in his socks.

They are so clean here, Sriram thought; in India the room would have been reeking of everyone's feet and the oil in their hair.

'... and Mr Khanna here is from India! What d'you think of America, Mr Khanna?' The professor beamed at him over his glasses. There was an expectant silence. Sriram looked around the ocean of faces and suddenly wished that someone would sweat. 'It's nice,' he stammered. 'I like it.'

Everyone kept asking him about America, how he liked it. How could he know if he liked it? He felt as if he wasn't really in America yet.

The supermarket would be a real American experience, he was sure. He went to Broadway Supermarket after class and walked in armed with his list.

The store was almost empty of customers; it was a Wednesday afternoon. Sriram glanced at the wall as he walked in and was startled to see his reflection in the glass. The slim brown young man pushing his empty cart looked so timidly back at him that he suddenly panicked. How was he going to fill up his cart? He had never gone shopping alone.

The first aisle had produce. He wheeled his cart in, looked around and stood stupefied. There was too much here, and no people. The gleaming bins of cucumbers, eggplants, lettuce, apples, walnuts, radishes looked so impeccable that he was afraid to touch them. The prices were set; there was no need to haggle with anyone. In some bins, each fruit had a separate price-tag.

Sriram instinctively took a deep breath, and smelled – nothing. He had the same sensation of surprise he'd had when once he had walked into a glass wall. He walked up to the parsley, lowered his head over it, and sniffed a couple of times. The parsley gave away nothing.

Sriram suddenly thought of Dadi-ma, of how her hands felt everything, how she touched and examined and sometimes tasted things before she bought them. Of how the vendors sometimes ran after her begging her to try just one guava, just one grape. Here there were no guavas and he didn't dare to taste a grape.

Under a sign that said 'Prickly Pears' were some reddish fruits that reminded him of guavas. He picked one up to smell but it communicated as little as the parsley had.

Sriram looked around furtively, then quickly jabbed his nail into the red flesh. He put the fruit back and inspected the pink goop on his finger. He looked around again and put the finger in his mouth. It wasn't guava.

He consulted his list, put everything he could find in his cart, and looked around the produce section one more time. Broccoli? What was that? He picked up a bunch and put it in the cart. Then he looked at a woman wheeling her cart toward him and saw that she had wrapped everything up in plastic. His fruits and vegetables, unbound, were jostling each other in his cart.

'What is this?' thought Sriram. 'Maybe it's against the law to allow all your fruits and vegetables to touch. Maybe it's unhygienic.' He watched the woman for a couple of minutes, and then began doing what she was doing – tearing off plastic bags from the rolls above the bins, and carefully putting each thing he picked into one.

After the produce, he proceeded to the bakery and then down every aisle in the store. One sign said, 'Health and Beauty Aids; Feminine.' He hesitated, torn between reticence and a desire to know what 'feminine' meant. He plunged in cart-first, to be confronted by an array of unguents, potions and sprays such as he had never imagined.

Stick deodorants, roll-on deodorants, spray deodorants, herb deodorants, unscented deodorants, soft deodorants, tough deodorants. Feminine spray deodorants. Where did they spray, wondered Sriram, thoroughly bemused. He read the directions on one can and decided that he would have to wait until his next grocery store trip to figure this out. Now he would get his cleaning supplies and go.

The cleaning supplies were quite confusing, as he couldn't decide what he needed. He could remember Dadi-ma buying Ajax powder to clean the toilet, the kitchen, everything. Here the array of choices was bewildering. Powder or scrubbing bubbles for the tub? Lysol spray for the walls or the mirror? And OdorEaters – where could one put them? And here was an object to stick on the wall and one to stick in the toilet tank. Sriram's head was spinning by this time and he took two or three large containers of Bon Ami powder off the shelf.

After a mental struggle in the 'Paper Goods' section, Sriram paid for his pile of purchases and walked home with his bags. The only time he had spoken was when he said 'Thank you' to the cashier for handing him his $4.63 change, and the sound of his own voice made his throat itch with unexpected forlornness.

After unloading his bags, he went for another class – Macroeconomic Theory. Here again, the professor went around the room asking for names and places of origin. There was another Indian in this class, a woman. Sriram looked at her and felt a mixture of relief and indignation. Why did she look so poised, and why was she dressed in Western clothes? She must be one of those fast girls from Cuffe Parade, one of Bombay's most *chi-chi* neighbourhoods.

'And what do you think of America?' The teaching fellow, a young woman, was asking Bharati, the Indian woman.

'Oh, I think it's very exciting to be here,' responded Bharati with a bright smile. 'Everyone is so open and friendly, and you can get to know people so easily.' Sriram glared at her. Did she use feminine deodorant spray, then, if she was so happy with America?

'And your fellow Indian? Mr Khanna? Do you feel the same way?'

Sriram opened his mouth to speak and discovered that frustration, bewilderment and loneliness were scratching his throat along with those unshed tears. He quickly shut his mouth, swallowed, and then opened it again to speak with an effort. 'America – I am happy to be here. It is very civilized, your country.'

After class, he fled to the bathroom in the hallway and leaned his head against the cool wall. Then he went into a stall and shut the door. Rummaging through his bag, he pulled out a long black object and looked at it for a moment.

Then he uncapped the highlighting pen, put down his bag, and started writing in fluorescent pink on the toilet stall wall. In small, firm letters, he wrote, 'In America, there are no smells'.

Mirchi-Ka-Salan (Chilli Curry)

4 oz fresh green chillis
5 to 6 curry leaves from an Indian shop
1 tbs cumin powder
1 tbs mustard seeds
4 tbs jaggery
2 tbs tamarind paste
salt to taste

Heat a little oil in a skillet [frying pan], put in the curry leaves, cumin and mustard seeds, and fry for half a minute. Add the de-seeded chillis. When it smells delicious, after about half a minute, take off the heat. Mix the jaggery and tamarind paste with salt and a little water. It should be thick and gooey and '*pacch-pacch*'. Add to the mixture in the skillet and fry everything together.

This is hot. It is a chutney to be eaten in small quantities with your meal; it is *not* meant to be a main course.

EDITOR'S NOTE

The juice in all capsicums (peppers) can make the skin sting and the eyes water. With chillis great care should be taken, washing the hands very thoroughly indeed after handling, as even a little can be very painful. In testing the recipe I had to use soft brown sugar instead of jaggery, and compressed tamarind instead of tamarind paste. These should be available in Asian shops. If using compressed tamarind for this recipe, pull off a piece about 2 inches (50 cm) square and soak in 1/4 pint (1/2 cup) of warm water for four hours or overnight. Then push this mixture through a fine sieve with a wooden spoon, adding a little water if necessary, and discarding the debris.

KATHY LETTE

Kathy Lette is Australian. At sixteen she shook
the school dust off her feet, and has since been
a cabaret artist, television satirist, playwright
and comedy writer in Hollywood, as well as
becoming a novelist. At the moment she lives
in London.

Buns are the Lowest Form of Wheat

KATHY LETTE

I AM renowned for my bad taste in interior decorating, infamous for lining tummies with fish fingers and creamed-regurgitated-from-can corn. Once I even went to the corner store and asked for a pinch of nutmeg and a clove of crushed garlic. If, like me, you think that 'aspic' is some posh ski resort in the Rockies, then read on.

This lack of culinary kudos is totally of my own making. Coming from a family of all girls, I found that every birthday brought another deposit of gift-wrapped aprons, garlic crushers and crock pots. My parents were determined to make us into 'good wife material'. In retaliation, I steadfastly refused to learn to cook. Never to be trapped into domesticity. Never to learn the art of home cooking. (You know, that place where a bloke thinks his girlfriend is.)

But eventually friends tire of a non-reciprocating guest. 'Must get together again soon,' my best friend farewelled me after my sixty-fifth meal in a row at her place. 'Have a nice decade.'

Shortly after, my half-baked boyfriend left me for a woman who owned a truffle slicer, melon baller and Mexican tortilla press. I concluded, after careful reasoning, that the answer was seasoning. The sexual revolution seems to be passé. Men are still only interested in gourmet and pâté. I *know*, I *know*. It's the Caring and Sharing 1990s. What happened to the Sensitive New Man who can do amazing things with mange-tout? Oh, he's like that initially. When you first meet him, the cuisinart is constantly on display; Elizabeth David cookbooks lie nonchalantly open on bedside tables. But once you move in, whenever he's in the vague vicinity of the kitchen, his arms seem mysteriously to atrophy . . .

Anyway, dining alone one night on Ryvitas trowelled in Vegemite, I decided there was no alternative. It was time to go into Hostess Mode ... The only hitch is that I grew up in laid-back Australia. We tend to take life with not just a pinch, but a packet of salt. I mean, if you accidentally burn a meal, you simply serve it up and call it 'Cajun'. If it's underdone then we eat 'sushi'. But the 'refained' English take their meal times much more seriously. Cooking my first dinner party for the members of the London literati turned out to be as gruelling as a Samurai initiation.

The torture began when I tried to plan a menu. The 1990s London palate has principles. For days I sat in pencil-gnawing puzzlement, trying to find some ideologically-sound ingredients. I ticked off the countries which would not win me any culinary kudos. Basically I couldn't use anything imported from Japan (whaling), Iran (mad mullahs), China (Tiananmen Square), Fiji (military dictatorship), Kenya, Sudan ... In the end, I was left with the most riveting ingredients: a few Nicaraguan coffee beans and New Zealand zucchini.

And that wasn't my only worry.

Two of the invited couples had told me that they were trying to conceive. One lot was trying for a boy and the other, a girl. According to the latest French research, to encourage the female gene, one must only eat tofu and bat's testes. Boy babies are best brought on with Tibetan fennel and Maltesers. Overcome with frustration, I just served pink food to one and blue to the other. And lemon for the first-time fatalists.

But planning a brilliant menu and preparing it beautifully doesn't guarantee a recipe for success. It's pointless giving painstaking thought to food, if you haven't given food to *thought*. The truth is, people are the most important ingredient. How often has your brain been double-glazed at a dinner party, by some newly-divorced bloke who suddenly feels the urge to tell you *all about it*? It's called whining and dining. You might as well be a full-length mirror.

For some reason, it's always the other end of the table which is riotous and laughter-laden. Unlike *my* end, where I'm seated between a Monitor of Continuous Flow goods and someone 'high up' in sewerage. (A connoisseur?) Directly opposite are two tone-poemists discussing their haemorrhoids. If only hosts could circulate to dinner party prospectives a menu selection of the other guests. Offering a choice, not of courses, but discourse. (After all, many a true word is spoken ingest.)

Well, *my* inaugural London literati bash would be different. I would decorate the table with LP's (Leading Publishers) and PTP's (Prominent Television Personalities) and RONWC's (Right-On New Wave Comedians). And sure enough, they got on like a stove on fire ... But as I slaved in the kitchen, balling melons and slicing truffles and pressing Mexican tortillas ...

I suddenly started to feel terribly like 'good wife material'. With not just one, but *seven* ravenous, raucous, tipsy and totally ungrateful husbands. The only time any of them paid me any attention was when the profiterole buns burnt and the chocolate syrup solidified. Voices stopped, mid-sentence. The atmosphere went icy. I thought I was going to be arrested, you know, for carrying a congealed weapon. When I pointed this out, the Right-On New Wave Comedian informed me coldly that 'puns are the lowest form of wit'. It was shortly afterwards that the Leading Publisher pushed away her untouched plate and announced that I'd done her a tremendous favour – she'd been contemplating a diet. Prominent Television Personality then departed with the comment that she was so glad I had taken her at her word and 'not gone to too much trouble'.

Too late I'd discovered the truth. The dinner party was invented as a form of torture. It proves, yet again, the endless capacity of human beings to inflict pain upon each other. Well, on the female of the species anyway. Dinner parties are a form of S and M (Sado Mastication).

So, it's back to Vegemite on Ryvitas. Still I have learnt one important lesson. The best thing you can possibly make for dinner, is a reservation. For one. Oh, and steer clear of profiteroles. Buns, after all, are the lowest form of wheat.

Recipe for Scratch and Sniff television

Remove Ryvita from packet. Must be corrugated and beige. The best ones resemble packing cardboard.

Smear on a cow's worth of butter.

Scrape on a veneer of Vegemite. Enough to give a little wake up call to the saliva glands, but not to terminate the life of the tonsils. (For those with a pallid palate, Marmite may be substituted.)

Leave to stand at room temperature, while you switch on the answering machine to fend off invitations to dull dinner parties.

Next, place feet comfortably on coffee table, aim remote control at television, tune into *Neighbours* (the Aussie revenge for Benny Hill and Harry Secombe) and take a big crunchy bite. It's a new invention. Scratch and Sniff television.

Margaret Drabble was born in Yorkshire, and
went to a Quaker school. One of Britain's
foremost novelists, she has also written studies
of Wordsworth and Arnold Bennett and edited
the *Oxford Companion to English Literature*.
She lives in London.

Diminishing Plenty

MARGARET DRABBLE

FOOD and the cooking of food have been the source of some of the most powerful anxieties of my life. I regularly have food nightmares from which I wake in terror – I dream that I present guests with boiled goldfish, that I have twelve to feed and nothing in the cupboard, that objects on the plate come alive and run around the table. Sometimes, more prosaically, I dream that I have bought a leg of lamb, and the dream is so realistic in every detail (though occasionally the butcher's shop is totally fictitious) that I believe through half the morning that the lamb is already in the refrigerator. Clearly I am not a relaxed or confident caterer.

While pondering what to attack in this contribution, I glanced for inspiration at my old friend Dusty Wesker's unconventional *Cookery Book*. It has recipes, but it also gives detailed accounts of real meals prepared for real people, and real things that may go wrong with them – a friend who is allergic to onions, sugar that refuses to caramelize, chicken terrine that doesn't slice properly, a rejected bread-and-butter pudding that may have reminded someone of school dinners. Dusty takes all these minor irritations in her stride. Over the years she has done a great deal of entertaining for her playwright husband Arnold, and she claims to enjoy it. She is, she admits, over-generous, often offering three choices of dessert, and she explains this in her foreword by saying that she was 'born poor and never learned how to be careful'. She is upset if people don't ask for seconds. I cannot exaggerate my admiration for this lavish, friendly, hospitable spirit. I would dearly love to share it. But even reading her book makes me feel anxious. I am a compulsive reader of cookery columns and they all make me feel anxious. I wish I could be cured of these fears. I wish I were more like Dusty, or more like another friend with a large family and a large house often full of guests that her husband has forgotten to say he has invited. She never bats an eyelid. Down they sit, politicians and academics and lawyers and novelists and children and lords and ladies, and eat what they are given, straight from the Aga. Sometimes it makes me want to weep at my own inadequacy.

I don't want to give the impression that I am a really bad cook, or that I don't like food. I enjoy eating, I can do some things quite well, and I like to see friends and family enjoying what I have prepared. But I continue to worry about it, and know I will never learn true insouciance. And naturally I am fascinated by the sources of my own obsessions.

I use descriptions of food a great deal in my fiction, because I think the way we cook and entertain – or fail to entertain – reveals a great deal about our characters. I may be dreaming again, but I think somebody once published a learned article on my works which concentrates on the symbolism of the Missing Cake which, it seems, my heroines never manage to provide for tea. I am particularly proud of two anxious cooks – both, significantly, lower-middle-class housewives brought up to believe that the successful dinner party will compensate for all other failures, intellectual, sexual or maternal. (Could these characters come from my eager schoolgirl reading of my mother's favourite magazine, *Woman*, with its little hints on how to lay tables and compose salads?) One of them, Janet Bird in *The Realms of Gold*, is seen preparing a feast of mushroom soup ('*One could not go wrong with mushroom soup, Di had told her, if one put enough sherry and cream in it. That was the kind of advice people were always giving her, and it was all very well, but sherry and cream were expensive . . .*'), which is to be followed by a new recipe for chicken with peaches. Janice Enderby, thirteen years later, in *A Natural Curiosity*, has graduated to chicken liver pâté with juniper berries, quails with braised cabbage and prunes, and lemon mousse: clearly in the Britain of the 1980s she has acquired a food processor and fancy notions, but she has not got rid of Janet's uncertainties. But in Janice, they have hardened into disgust.

Many novelists enjoy writing about dinner parties, disastrous and otherwise, and it is by no means a female or feminist preserve. There is far more culinary detail in Zola and Proust than in Jane Austen (whose own preserves, one suspects, may well have been horrible, like the porridge and potatoes of the poor Brontës and the mutton pies of Dorothy Wordsworth, which make one's nostrils stop and one's teeth ache two centuries later). Dickens and Trollope give us some superb descriptions of ill-judged social gatherings. Particularly delightful and reassuring are the inept efforts of the upwardly mobile David Copperfield to entertain and impress, first as a bachelor about town, then as a young-married man. On the first occasion, his landlady having refused to attend to anything but potatoes, he sends out for vast quantities of food from the pastry cook (some of which mysteriously shrinks in the preparation) and employs a youth and a young woman to wait: he eagerly opens far too many bottles of wine, and ends up with one of the most magnificent hangovers ever described. On the second, he and child-wife Dora order a barrel of oysters – but have no idea how to open them. And whose heart does not go out to Trollope's young couple who plan a quiet, jolly, informal wedding eve celebration for immediate old friends and family, but find themselves adding to the gathering unnecessary relatives and courses, culminating in some highly-coloured round cakes from that lethally-tempting pastry cook? They know they are making mistakes, they know a simple meal of roast lamb would have been much more acceptable and enjoyable to all concerned, but they cannot help themselves, they are led on by a dangerous mixture of goodwill and ambition to destruction.

This is all rich material for writer and reader, and makes one honour all the more those who can feed others confidently. I suspect that my own troubles stem from my mother. She did not like to cook for anyone outside the family, because of her own profound social insecurities, and I remember terrible scenes with my father on the rare occasions when he prevailed upon her to invite any of his colleagues to dinner. (Friends he had none, or only one; she wouldn't let him.) Hysterics and bitter anger would cloud the house for days before, to be dispelled in disarming mildness as soon as the feared interloper arrived. Yet my mother was a good cook – far better in her prime than I have ever been – and had nothing to worry about. Her roasts and poultry, her Yorkshire puddings, her cakes and pastries were all excellent. And she was also quite adventurous: she would launch merrily out on a lobster from our trusty Sheffield fishmonger, and was game to struggle with aubergines and garlic.

In later years, her cooking deteriorated, as she and my father ate less and more carefully. Or was it perhaps the food itself that got worse, or one's memory that glorified the roast goose, the lemon puddings of yesteryear? I think the flavour and quality of meat have deteriorated very significantly, which goes some way to explaining why more and more of us are vegetarians, and why even good cooks fear the tough or tasteless (and very expensive) piece of beef. But I think this sense of diminishing plenty is something that many of us associate with the failing powers of our parents. When I was a child, our home may not have been hospitable, or happy, but at least we within it all ate well, in stark contrast to school food and the food cooked by some of my friends' families. So we could think of it as a nourishing place. Revisiting, as a young and then middle-aged adult with a home and children of my own, and with my own culinary preferences, I began to find it less and less sustaining. I recall a particularly nasty jar of instant powdered coffee, and my mother's astonishment when I dared to point out that the reason why it wasn't, as she admitted, very nice, was that it was a cheap and nameless brand. Oh, do they taste different? she innocently enquired. Food is power, and the power was passing to us. (My elder sister, incidentally, is a very good cook: in 1960 she gave me a heap of cookery books as a wedding present, which may or may not account for something. I certainly feel I have never lived up to them.)

There is a poignant description of this power-passing in Angelica Garnett's heartbreaking account of her childhood as daughter of Vanessa Bell and Duncan Grant, *Deceived by Kindness*. She recalls the generous hospitality at Charleston in Sussex, where her mother (in sharp contrast with her much more anxious and nervous sister Virginia Woolf) dispensed good food and painted fruits and flowers and bottles of wine – heroic days, which have become an image of plenty for many of us who never knew it at first-hand. Then, returning as an adult, Angelica found her magical parents mysteriously aged and diminished, and the refrigerator empty. Gone were the feasts, shrivelled the bloom of the fruits, and overgrown the kitchen garden. It is a peculiarly powerful transformation scene, which not only reduces the parents to mortal size, but makes them retrospectively vulnerable. And it is largely done, or at least in my recollection, through the image of that empty refrigerator.

So, how do I cope with my kitchen neuroses? First of all, I exorcise them by writing about them, which helps me and I hope comforts others. I don't let them get in the way of seeing friends and family. I swallow my 1960s Superwoman pride and occasionally employ caterers or order, like David Copperfield but I hope more judiciously, from our local delicatessen. I never – or hardly ever – make a pudding. And I tend to stick to nice safe meals which don't require last minute attention or frequent visits to the kitchen. (I hate being watched while I cook, largely because most of the time I don't know what I am doing, and I worry that people will notice. This means that I am also very hard to assist.) So here is a recipe for lemon chicken which really cannot go very wrong. (Chickens *never* go as wrong as lamb or beef or potatoes. Potatoes can be a real disaster. I have never mastered the potato.)

Lemon Chicken

Roast or boil a chicken until it is done. If you don't know how long that is – well, neither do I. You just have to keep an eye on it and prod it when you think it is about the right time.

Wait for it to cool. Make a pint of sauce with butter, cornflour, and a mixture of milk and juice from the chicken. (No fat off the chicken, though.) Then add to the white sauce the juice of one or two lemons and, if you wish, one of those nice chicken stock cubes. You can also add cream if in the mood. Then joint the chicken or take it all off the bones and put it in a fireproof dish and pour the sauce over it. This can then be gently reheated at will. Serve with rice which may be enlivened by pine nuts or almonds, or anything you think goes with lemon and chicken. You may or may not wish to serve with a green vegetable. Or a green salad. I never know which I am going to do. But I do assure you that this dish cannot be really awful. Good luck.

Margaret Atwood is Canadian, an internationally-renowned novelist, short-story writer and poet. She spent much of her early life in the northern Ontario and Quebec bush country. She now lives in Toronto.

'Bread'
From: *Murder in the Dark*

MARGARET ATWOOD

IMAGINE a piece of bread. You don't have to imagine it, it's right here in the kitchen, on the bread board, in its plastic bag, lying beside the bread knife. The bread knife is an old one you picked up at an auction; it has the word BREAD carved into the wooden handle. You open the bag, pull back the wrapper, cut yourself a slice. You put butter on it, then peanut butter, then honey, and you fold it over. Some of the honey runs out onto your fingers and you lick it off. It takes you about a minute to eat the bread. This bread happens to be brown, but there is also white bread, in the refrigerator, and a heel of rye you got last week, round as a full stomach then, now going mouldy. Occasionally you make bread. You think of it as something relaxing to do with your hands.

Imagine a famine. Now imagine a piece of bread. Both of these things are real but you happen to be in the same room with only one of them. Put yourself into a different room, that's what the mind is for. You are now lying on a thin mattress in a hot room. The walls are made of dried earth and your sister, who is younger than you are, is in the room with you. She is starving, her belly is bloated, flies land on her eyes; you brush them off with your hand. You have a cloth too, filthy but damp, and you press it to her lips and forehead. The piece of bread is the bread you've been saving, for days it seems. You are as hungry as she is, but not yet as weak. How long does this take? When will someone come with more bread? You think of going out to see if you might find something that could be eaten, but outside the streets are infested with scavengers and the stink of corpses is everywhere.

Should you share the bread or give the whole piece to your sister? Should you eat the piece of bread yourself? After all, you have a better chance of living, you're stronger. How long does it take to decide?

Imagine a prison. There is something you know that you have not yet told. Those in control of the prison know that you know. So do those not in control. If you tell, thirty or forty or a hundred of your friends, your comrades, will be caught and will die. If you refuse to tell, tonight will be like last night. They always choose the night. You don't think about the night however, but about the piece of bread they offered you. How long does it take? The piece of bread was brown and fresh and reminded you of sunlight falling across a wooden floor. It reminded you of a bowl, a yellow bowl that was once in your home. It held apples and pears; it stood on a table you can also remember. It's not the hunger or the pain that is killing you but the absence of the yellow bowl. If you could only hold the bowl in your hands, right here, you could withstand anything, you tell yourself. The bread they offered you is subversive, it's treacherous, it does not mean life.

There were once two sisters. One was rich and had no children, the other had five children and was a widow, so poor that she no longer had any food left. She went to her sister and asked her for a mouthful of bread. 'My children are dying,' she said. The rich sister said, 'I do not have enough for myself,' and drove her away from the door. Then the husband of the rich sister came home and wanted to cut himself a piece of bread; but when he made the first cut, out flowed red blood.

Everyone knew what that meant.

This is a traditional German fairy-tale.

The loaf of bread I have conjured for you floats about a foot above your kitchen table. The table is normal, there are no trap doors in it. A blue tea towel floats beneath the bread, and there are no strings attaching the cloth to the bread or the bread to the ceiling or the table to the cloth, you've proved it by passing your hand above and below. You didn't touch the bread though. What stopped you? You don't want to know whether the bread is real or whether it's just a hallucination I've somehow duped you into seeing. There's no doubt that you can see the bread, you can even smell it, it smells like yeast, and it looks solid enough, solid as your own arm. But can you trust it? Can you eat it? You don't want to know, imagine that.

RANA KABBANI

Rana Kabbani was born in Damascus to a
Muslim family. She grew up in New York and
Djakarta, and was educated in the United States
and Britain. A writer and academic, she now
lives in London.

Dada Fatima's Kitchen

RANA KABBANI

IT WAS a small kitchen, as I discovered to my surprise when I returned to visit it many years later. It had seemed endlessly elastic in those days, certainly capable of encompassing everything I would ever learn of the world

She would arrive at eight every morning, dusty ..om the congested two-hour bus-ride that brought her from the dirt-poor village of Jobar where she lived to my grandmother's flat in Damascus. Her first ten minutes would always be spent undressing. First she unpinned her gauzy black face-veil, transferring the pins from her mouth to a magnet stuck to the fridge. Then she whipped off her demure, hand-me-down coat and black patent shoes, rolled down her garters and dun-coloured stockings, slipped on some flowery pantaloons and a long flowing skirt, wrapped her plaited grey hair with a white cotton veil, put her bare feet in their old wooden clogs, all the while calling on God to cheer her spirits along.

Then she would kiss me, nine little pecks on my right cheek, nine little pecks on my left, and from a paper bag extract that morning's surprise: a yolk-coloured chick that would soon 'fall asleep' with its minute feet in the air; musky green walnuts that turned my fingernails black; beetles that glowed in the dark of their boxes, salt lupins in newspaper cones; a kitten so small it curled up to rest in the tiny saucer it ate from; a necklace of jasmine that dripped shiny ants.

Dada Fatima was sixty then, but her cheeks were pink and firm like sugar apples and her body was as fit as a girl's. She had had several husbands; the first she'd married at twelve, hugging her ragdolls for comfort on the night of the 'entry'. Nothing since then had caused her to alter her low opinion of men. Abu al-Fawz, the last of her spouses, had taken to living in the

73

uppermost branches of a mulberry tree to escape from her blows.

'That no-good donkey', she'd shout, as she gave my mother a daily report of his doings. 'Rabbits! He now wants to breed goddamn rabbits!' And so would flow stories of schemes that always ended in tears. No purchasers turned up to buy rabbits, which multiplied into the hundreds and ran amok through the village, ravaging vegetable plots. With two bottles of home-distilled arak, Abu al-Fawz took to his hammock, and left her to pay for the damage.

At nine, Fatima set the Primus stove going, and began her morning routine of trying to decide what to cook. The barrel boys passed beneath the kitchen verandah, hawking their wares: 'Artichokes! Corn! Dewdrunk corn!', they would cry. 'How much is the kilo?' she'd ask. 'Seventy *piastres*.' 'Seventy *piastres*? Crooks! Robbers! Have you no shame? Thirty-five is more than you're getting! Bring me up two and a half kilos as fast as your legs will run!'

Next came the milk-man with his string of she-goats who clattered up the stone steps and entered the kitchen's back door. 'Maaa, maaa, maaaa,' they shivered as their teats were pulled to fill an aluminium pail with foam. The milk had to be boiled for an hour. Once it had cooled, a thick yellow skin appeared on its surface, and this was scooped up in an old slotted spoon and placed on a dish before me. Sprinkled with gritty white sugar, I ate it with unleavened bread.

One winter, I became ill with hepatitis and spent a few weeks in bed. I can still feel Fatima's chapped hand on my forehead, feeling for fever. She would force soup down my throat, never taking no for an answer. 'Food is for eating, my girl! Eat it if you can get it! Not everyone can get it!' These words would invariably introduce one of her 'my poor neighbour' stories. She had gone to see her poor neighbour (went one that clings ferociously to my mind) and had found her brewing a brown smelly mixture in her only pot. 'What is this?' Fatima had asked her. 'It is soup for my sick daughter,' the woman had answered. 'And what is it made of?', Fatima wanted to know. 'Why, shit! It's made of shit. Seeing whatever I feed her comes out the other end, I thought I'd do better to spoon it back in! Times are hard and food is scarce, and my other little ones have to eat.' Fatima would pause to gauge the effect of her story, and find that I'd stiffened under the covers, and that tears of horror had sprung to my eyes. 'Stop your snivelling, monkey,' she'd say in her matter of fact way, 'When did the poor have a choice?'

Fatima was obsessive about cleanliness, and would pour scorn on the washing strung out on the neighbourhood lines. *She* boiled whites till they were threadbare, and ran through more washing-blue in a month than most people used in a year. And because of these high standards, it was invariably she who found a hair in the store-bought pudding, or the gross remains of a fly. Store-bought meant dirt in her book, and only homemade would do.

Huge amounts of produce would arrive in the kitchen: sixty kilos of dog-apricots which needed de-stoning for that year's batch of jam; twelve crates of tomatoes to boil down for paste; mountains of olives for curing in brine.

The year that I was seven she asked me to help her with the eggplant sorting. Three men had hauled up an immense canvas bag filled to bursting, which Fatima had slit down the middle with her favourite knife. Out they had fallen: eggplant in all shapes and sizes – smooth, elongated purple ones, wrinkled baby blue ones, white ones that curved up like ivory tusks, black ones with bitter brown seeds in their cottony flesh. Each kind served a purpose, and it was joked that no self-respecting man would travel abroad during eggplant season, or marry a wife unable to cook it in eight dozen ways – fried, grilled, baked, stewed, stuffed, smothered in sauce, slivered in lamb, simmered in broth, sat on a bed of yoghurt and herbs, candied in syrup, pickled in salt, and on, and on, and on.

'Make a pile of the small green ones for your old dada,' Fatima commanded, as she hitched up her skirts and squatted on the tiled floor, sorting the various colours. 'Look, look what I found!' I said, pointing at three, minute, pink-coloured eggplants stuck close together. Fatima bent forward to see, and then began screaming as though her hair had caught fire: 'Mice! Mice! Unclean beasts! God save my soul from unclean things!' With a bit of rag she took hold of the small creatures, and ran out onto the verandah, even forgetting to don her veil in her agitation. She threw the rag away from her as far as she could fling it, and it landed on top of a garage where the tom cats lived, its contents exposed to their hunger. Running back into the kitchen like someone possessed, she began pouring disinfectant permanganate crystals into buckets of water, and dumping the hundreds of eggplants in this bright purple bath, where they bobbed up and down for the night.

Some evenings, in this country that I must now consider home, I sit in the dark watching my son and daughter sleep. I catch myself humming the sad lullaby that Fatima used to sing to me all those years ago. I think of her, dead so many years, all her labour spent. And my spirit becomes heavy, heavy as that vanished child's, listening to her singing voice.

Baba Ghannuj (Eggplant Dip)

Take three large eggplants or aubergines, and set them, one at a time, atop the naked flame of a gas stove. Turn them gradually (holding them by the tail, which should jut away from the fire) till they are entirely charred and shrunken soft inside.

Place them in a sieve, sprinkle a little salt on them, and let them cool for fifteen minutes. Then scoop out the flesh with a spoon, discarding the burnt black skin and the tail. Put this smoky flesh in a largish, shallow bowl, and with a fork, mash it vigorously till you have a smoothish cream.

Add two tbs of good olive oil to this, as well as one clove of garlic directly from the garlic press, and one tbs of Greek strained yoghurt. Beat them all together once again.

Serve this Syrian dip with warmed-up bread, preferably the flat, unleavened kind.

EDITOR'S NOTE

Although a gas flame (or, better still, a hot charcoal grill or barbecue) gives the slight smokiness which characterises this dish at its best, the aubergines (eggplants) can be charred and softened under a hot grill (broiler), though it takes longer. They should be turned so that they blacken all over. Readers who have already encountered aubergine (eggplant) dip, sometimes known as 'Aubergine Caviar', will notice that this recipe calls for no onion or lemon juice and comparatively little salt. The result is very subtle.

BENOÎTE GROULT

Benoîte Groult was born in Paris. One of France's leading feminist writers she is, besides being a novelist, a distinguished journalist, and has adapted fiction for television. Passionate about fishing, she divides her time between Paris, Hyères, Brittany and Ireland.

La Mer à la Cuisine

BENOÎTE GROULT
Translated by ANTONIA TILL

'WHAT'S for dinner tonight?' Just one little phrase, yet single-handed it has alienated more women from cooking than any feminist tract, than all the hours of dutiful toil, all the myriad problems of life today. It's not the phrase itself which is so deadly, it's the way it's reiterated over days, months, years . . . And the addition of 'darling' to the formula ('Darling, what are you giving us tonight?') only sinks us deeper in the ugly suspicion that cooking is seen as no more than a way of proving our love for the family, the corollary being that a woman who doesn't enjoy cooking convicts herself of outrageous egoism, soon construed as lack of love for her family.

She needs to undergo a long apprenticeship to egoism, one of women's finest victories this century, in order to escape this emotional blackmail and convince her household (whose vested interest lies in maintaining the confusion) that the necessity to provide every day must not be confused with true cooking, which is personal taste, an art, at its most extreme a major life-choice. She needs to be ready to make a series of demands which, since the price of liberty is high, are likely to be wounding, before the kitchen can be transformed from the furrow a woman is condemned to ploughing for life, to one of the most sophisticated rooms in the house, the place where people are most likely to congregate. It's in the kitchen that confidences are exchanged, that family life takes place; it's among the remains of a meal or when you're elbow-deep in peelings that you ask yourself what life is all about, rather than when you're sunk in an armchair in the sitting room.

Alas, exploiting the guilt, the exhaustion, this lack of time which working women know too well, the food industry has taken upon itself the role of kitchen genie. It has flooded the market with ready-cooked meals of such variety as to dishearten even the most inventive housewife. True, the pastry of those plastic-wrapped supermarket pies, life-sized versions of dolls' -house food, is never burnt; the stews never stick to the bottoms of their polystyrene containers; the powdered soups, poured from their vacuum packs, offer no surprises. It's precisely this mediocrity of sameness, this lack of any surprise in texture or taste, which gradually makes the consumer feel that feeding is nothing but a physiological necessity, something to be got over as quickly as possible. You only have to be fuelled (it couldn't be described as eating) 30,000 feet up, by economy-class airline caterers, to recognize the utter dreariness of these dead victuals on their plastic trays. If we don't watch out, the pleasure to be gained from the discriminating enjoyment of food will be lost. It may not be long before the art of fine cooking is viewed as the invention of a handful of snobs, mere sybaritic luxury. People will forget that true conviviality can only flourish during a good meal lovingly prepared, that good food and wine quicken the intelligence, mellow the mood and stimulate conversation. A whole aspect of living well, of civilization itself, is threatened with extinction.

The obsession with slimming doesn't help. We've seen the advent of products characterized in terms of calories, digestion time, lipids, proteins, glycids. The joyous Laughing Cow of the cheese advertisements, the rubicund monk on Camembert boxes, the fatty bacon of our pigs, all stand accused. The ultimate aim is to label these sorry products as aerated, skimmed, fat-free, the highest achievement to declare them 0%. When zero becomes a mark of value in food something must be amiss. To crown it all, we now have the microwave oven which can cook food in seconds without so much as heating the dish, and which makes kitchens, the most earthy places, the most comforting cocoons, seem like infernal laboratories.

But it looks as if the new 'green' mood, the fashion for old houses, traditional kitchens and regional produce, might be a way of rescuing the art of cooking. We're discovering that it's not so much a question of digging out our grandmothers' recipes, of recalling the unrivalled flavour of the food we had as children, as a question of reasserting our identity, indeed of conserving our birthright. Nowadays, with European bureaucrats threatening cultural homogenization, cooking is a way of affirming our differences. When we're faced with the invasion by McDonald's, it becomes a form of resistance. Faced with the anonymous potato they want to impose from Dunkirk to Marseille, we rediscover the true nature of things if we can tell the difference between a Belle de Fontenay or a Roseval and what is depressingly known as an 'eating potato'.

Medical journals have recently published a most heartening study carried out in Finland. It was conducted with 500 volunteers aged between forty and fifty to establish the connection between cardio-vascular disease and cholesterol. Half of them were subjected to a strict regime for five years, with appropriate medical treatment followed by regular check-ups, and a healthy life-style with no alcohol or tobacco. The others were left to carry on with their lives, eating and drinking as usual, and being given no special treatment. When the five years were up, the Finnish doctors, to their eternal credit, announced that the group which had been medically supervised showed more deaths from heart disease, higher cholesterol levels and depressive symptoms; there had even been a suicide. The study showed that the people who did best were the men and women who had been allowed to live carefree lives, which must be an indication that a light heart and a capacity for enjoyment – of good food among other things – are the surest antidotes to hardening of the arteries.

Soupe de Crevettes

This finding authorizes me to offer you a recipe which, provided that you follow every instruction to the letter, affords the most perfect pleasure from first to last. Admittedly you could omit the first two steps, but the final result would have less intensity of flavour, and it would be harder to find all the ingredients. So I'll begin at the beginning.

Buy yourself a small island off the West coast of Ireland or, failing that, one of the Chausey islands, the only place in France where fishing is still miraculous, and the only Channel Islands which haven't been hijacked by perfidious Albion.

Acquire a current tide-table for the area, to find out the dates and times of the spring (highest) tides each fortnight.

Carefully choose some promising rocks and place some *casiers* [lobster pots] around them so that they will be under water at high tide. Or you could take a shrimping net and wade among the seaweed, preferably the wide flat ribbony kind, at low tide. Keep fishing until the tide turns two hours later.

Returning to the cottage with which you have thoughtfully furnished yourself on the island, pour yourself a glass of vodka. Now settle down to enjoy the 2 lb or so of glorious seafood which you will have harvested, and which you eat warm after cooking it in seawater for three minutes. Reserve all the prawns and shrimps, large or small.

Now embark on the recipe – *soupe de crevettes*. If you have 12 oz or more, it will be enough for four. Toss the little crustaceans, live, in hot oil in a large, heavy pan. When they have all turned pink, pour over a small glass of Calvados and set it alight, shaking the pan until the flames die down. Whisky (Scotch or Irish) will do, but doesn't impart such a good flavour. Add almost 2 pints of water, one or two sliced carrots, an onion, a leek, both sliced, and a small tin of tomato purée. Season with *gros sel* [coarse rock or sea salt], pepper, cayenne, allspice and one or two whole cloves, a pinch of thyme and a bay leaf. Bring to the boil and skim. In another pan, make a white *roux* with flour and a little of the hot liquid, and add it to the soup to make the texture velvety. Simmer for half an hour.

Here we come to the most delicate part of the operation, extracting all the goodness of the shellfish and vegetables while getting rid of the shells. Either press as much as possible through a sieve, using a pestle or chunky wooden spoon, or put it all through a *mouli-légumes*. This will give you a smooth bisque of a uniform colour, shrimp pink. Adjust the seasoning and, just before serving, add a small pot of *crème fraîche*, or whipping cream sharpened with a dessertspoonful of lemon juice. Serve the soup piping hot, with croûtons if you like. Your guests will never guess what it is: *soupe de crevettes* tastes quite different from crab or lobster bisque or crayfish soup. Its flavour is unforgettable.

It's just possible to make this soup with a pound or so of those assorted shrimps you can net among the rocks at high tide, in which case you could manage without the island.

But that would be an awful shame!

Molly Keane ('M.J. Farrell') was born in Co. Kildare, Ireland, to 'a rather serious Hunting and Fishing Churchgoing family', and adopted a pseudonym for her first ten novels. After a long gap she resumed writing under her own name. She lives in Eire.

From: Nursery Food

MOLLY KEANE

I was born in 1904, and by 1908 I had accepted the fact that nursery food
was so disgusting that greed, even hunger, must be allayed elsewhere.

In my childhood there was little or no communication between the
nurseries, at the top of the house, and the kitchen, three flights of stairs
beneath in the basement. Nanny and Mrs Finn, the cook, had no liking for
each other. Nanny, considering herself socially superior, would send Mrs
Finn acid messages via the nursery maid (with meagre effect) on the quality
or quantity of the food that travelled up on black tin trays wreathed with
roses for nursery breakfast, dinner and tea. Today, given there was a nanny,
and a cook, Nanny would have enough sense to crawl to the cook – but not
at that date.

As a result of such exclusive behaviour and an enmity unimaginable
today, we children grew weedy and green and greedy, forever in search of
food to supplement our nursery fare. Indoors and out, given, found or
stolen, we looked for food we could enjoy

I think still of breakfasts in the cold day-nursery: porridge, classically full
of lumps, eaten out of small brown bowls with Scotch mottoes on their
yellow insides – 'Keep your breath to cool your Parritch' – why not
'porridge'? we wondered. After porridge, bread and butter, and a mug (with
your name on it) of milk. Boiled eggs were for Sundays or birthdays.
Breakfast over, we were dressed to go out, Nanny speeding the button-hook
mercilessly down the length of a fat leg. No doubt she was glad to see the
last of my brother and me, and then turn gratefully to a quiet cup of tea
before bathing the baby, towels already spread to warm on the high,
brass-rimmed fender.

Once away from the nursery, there was little or no surveillance of myself, aged five, or of my brother, a mature seven. We were free in our outdoor country world, and as inclined towards misbehaviour as any rampaging mob in a city slum. The mornings started with a stampede down flights of stairs from nursery to kitchen – the back stairs, of course, for children and staff. We clattered down the wooden slope before the descent of the twisted stone stairway to the basement and the hot kitchen, a world away from nursery life.

The kitchen was a place full of drama and shouting, for Mrs Finn was temperamental. Sometimes we were welcomed with kisses, much dreaded on account of the strong growth of her beard. On her day off, Mrs Finn would retire to her bedroom to shave and to practise her fiddle. The air of a jig – 'The Pride of Erin' or 'Johnnie, When You Die' – would creep hesitantly down the house; she was not very expert.

What did submission to her kisses buy us? Rashers, forgotten on top of the range, their fat crisped away to paper; a broken meringue, creamless; a buttered crust dipped heavily in sugar; sugar in a twist of paper, to carry away and lick in the hay-loft. Now and then it was lumps of cane coffee-sugar, with a fine string running through their amber rocks, or prunes out of a blue, bruised paper bag (grocery bags were thick as blotting paper then, plastic undreamed of).

I can think of no moment of gastronomic tension better relaxed and fulfilled than on those morning raids, timed to the preparation of dining-room breakfast. Then we would wait and watch while the fat cook, her skirts to the floor, black boot-toes peeping out below, would split the breakfast scone she held in one hand, then scrape both halves on the hot frying-pan before she clapped them together again with half a rasher of bacon between.

'Off now,' she would shout, 'and don't let anyone see yee! That one above will kill the three of us.' She meant Nanny. It was her hatred of Nanny that made her, apart from nursery meals, such an able confederate. We brought her our outdoor spoils to cook: minnows she classed as dirty, poisonous and tedious to gut, so we were forced to abandon these forerunners of whitebait. But she would boil our bantam's eggs, and cut fingers of bread-and-butter small enough for us to dip in them; or toast mushrooms on top of the Eagle range, a little salt and butter in their hollows.

Hungry or not, we looked for food out of doors, and were serious in our intention of finding it. In the farmyard, where we fed our pigeons, bantams and prolific white rabbits, we would lean and heave our joint weight on the heavy wheel that sliced carrots and mangolds for the milking cows; the coarse-shavings of carrots crunched enticingly between our teeth. Carrots and the blue fluff in my coat pocket are always together in my mind.

In the walled kitchen garden, stricter watch was kept on us. Jim Geoghan, the lame gardener, could ignore disturbances louder than any blackbird made under gooseberry bushes or netted white strawberries; he could forget us in the moist glooms and shades of the raspberry canes. It was the eye of our resident maiden aunt, a dedicated and diligent gardener, that we most feared. Sometimes Aunt Marjorie would say, 'Now, children. Five minutes in the raspberry patch,' and then stand, watch in hand (it hung on a gold chain round her neck, a blue enamel-backed watch, ornamented with a diamond dove) while we ate as much as we could, as fast as we were able. Although we did not know the time, we knew she called us out before five minutes were up.

Aunt Marjorie was not always in the garden to pounce on us and forbid – on winter mornings we felt free to poke potatoes into the heart of a bonfire. While weeds simmered and smoked above them, we would ride away on our donkeys to ditches full of watercress, returning to a midday feast of roast potatoes, red-hot and floury inside their charcoal jackets. Cooled by wet cresses in the mouth, no potatoes have ever been so good. We gobbled them in the streaky shade of the nut-walk, where, months earlier, we had stripped the pointed green cauls off the filberts and hazelnuts that grew so tidily and secretly on their stems.

Adventures of disobedience were always available to put an extra edge on our forays. On Saturdays (Jim Geoghan's day off) the garden was locked against us, Aunt Marjorie holding the key. In the season of mists and mellow fruitfulness this was a shocking deprivation; but then, stolen fruit is best of all.

One autumn Saturday, before Aunt Marjorie was stirring, my brother Charles and I hurried up the laurel-shaded path to the kitchen garden, wet, blue hydrangea heads buffeting us as we ran. He did not tell me what we were going to do. I knew. And I feared for him. I waited under the Portugal laurels while Charles climbed on the uncertain swag of their branches to achieve the immense height of the garden wall. From far above the solid green door, with its great, vacant keyhole, I can still see his pale face under the sailor hat, 'HMS Majestic' on its ribbon, as he looked down to me. 'Don't chance it, Charlie!' I called. 'You'll be killed!' He turned his little green face away from me – from a woman's clinging and fear – and jumped. Half a lifetime afterwards when he rode round Liverpool and faced Becher's, did the same decision uphold him? For better or for worse, you cannot say no to Becher's. On this morning, more frightening than any field of horses, Aunt Marjorie was behind to jump on him.

After the thud of a body landing, then a pause while I wondered if he was dead, the first apple soared over the wall and fell, pale and golden, at my feet. Others followed, some more green than gold. I gathered them up, five or six or seven, and stuffed them into the elasticated legs of my blue knickers. Charles's approval of their safe disposal thrilled me with pride – it was male approbation at its earliest manifestation.

When he rejoined me, with the help of a ladder from the toolshed, we jogged along hand in hand through the morning – a bluish tinge of earliest autumn in the air – to the ivy-smothered butt of a small ruined watchtower, our favourite place for consuming food or hiding treasures. Rooks and gulls sped over the roofless square of stone, where the past kept its secrets, and the secrets of our present hour were safe.

Susie Orbach was born in the United Kingdom. She is a feminist psychotherapist, active in the women's movement, and helped to found the Women's Therapy Centre. Her writing focuses on women's psychology and emotions. She lives in London.

A Language all of its Own

SUSIE ORBACH

S ANDRA, a twenty-four-year-old nurse on an acute cancer ward, collapses from fatigue. She's been working almost ceaselessly and under great pressure for eighteen months. Everyone sees her as an enormously caring and capable young woman who goes out of her way to make her patients as comfortable as possible, who watches that the doctors get their decimal points in the right place when prescribing, who ministers to the grieving family and friends of her patients. She's a model nurse, a model woman, a model carer. Selfless, conscientious and kind, her collapse engenders surprise and concern.

Sandra's collapse was caused by starvation. Voluntary starvation. Sandra lived in a nightmarish contradiction of providing the essential care needed for others to regain their health, while depriving herself of the most basic means of keeping going herself. Like many other young women in the West – so many that we would rather not know – Sandra has been denying herself food for years.

It started when she was eleven years old. She enacted a ritual she believed to do with her approaching adult femininity. She started dieting. Following her older sisters and her mother, her attitude towards food became mercurial. Food took on the status of magic and naughtiness on the one hand, and tempter and punisher on the other. From being encouraged to eat along with her brothers and father, Sandra now experienced subtle pressure from her mother and sisters to be wary of food, to be watchful of what she ate, to evaluate the food she desired and the food that entered her body. Talk at home seemed to revolve around diet foods, slimming regimes, appearance and weight. Where she had felt reasonably carefree about her body and about eating as a little girl, her appearance, her weight, her food intake came to dominate much of her experience.

Her schoolfriends were no less preoccupied than she. Conversations with peers always included a reference to eating and dieting. Together they schemed to find the best way to become/stay slim. None of them had a straightforward relationship to food (that is to say: to eat when hungry and stop when full). They were all involved in some deprivation schema or other, most commonly the elimination of particular foods and the over-riding of appetite. But this self-imposed stricture brought with it painful acts of rebellion. The young women found themselves in the bakery or at the refrigerator stuffing food into their mouths as fast as they could; eating so quickly and so guiltily that they barely tasted it; learning to induce vomiting or evacuation as though to do away with what had been taken in.

Food for these First World girls and women had become extremely dangerous territory. They fantasized about pills that would turn them off food, pills that would negate what they ate, pills that would make them into the size they wanted to be. Alongside this terror of food and their desperate attraction to it, lay an even – to non-Western eyes – more curious phenomenon. Sandra, her friends, sisters and mother, along with countless other women, accepted at some level this stance towards food. In other words it didn't strike them as peculiar. They took it on as part and parcel of being female. They expected to diet for life, to be burdened by a fear of food, to feel guilty about their appetites, to chase one scheme after another to control their eating. In the course of their week they would read endless 'advice' in magazines, newspapers and books about diet, appearance, weight, exercise, body image. This was the normality they subscribed to.

And therein lies the crime.

Sandra collapses from the effects of self-starvation. But, predicated on guilt about eating, the *normative* response of Western women to food ranges from compulsive eating, to bingeing and to starving. Sandra is, sadly, not so much the oddity, but the exemplification of an attitude towards food by girls and women in our culture.

Food for many women is not only tantalizing and terrifying as I have suggested, it also symbolizes much of their relationship to the world. While food is something women routinely prepare and give to others, and in that context experience themselves as providing love, nourishment, nurture and care, for themselves food is dangerous, virtually off-limits, or at the very least to be feared. This is tragically analogous to their position in Western culture where a woman has been designated to be midwife to others' activities – her husband's, her children's – to be the person who makes it possible for those around her to function and partake of the world, to nurture them emotionally, service them domestically, support them in their needs and desires, while not expecting reciprocal support. The world, like food, is scarcely for her. Even in 1992, twenty years or so after the beginning of the second wave of feminism, women and women's values are only reluctantly received by our world.

Women demanding a place in the world outside the domestic encounter prejudice of the most insidious nature. They are continually sexualized, their contributions often experienced as threatening; they are unsupported. They have to be more adequate than their male counterparts, but make sure they don't show it; they have to bury the domestic responsibilities they carry lest they be thought unserious on the job; they have to define themselves in relation to standards they weren't part of creating and, added to all this, they are required to pay enormous attention to that marker of femininity – their appearance. If they enter the workforce (which of course most of them/us do) they need to import that stigma of female oppression, a preoccupation with meeting the prevailing dress and body standards of the day which inevitably involve a degree of obsessive concern for food and weight.

While there was a certain logic – although a deeply offensive and ugly logic – about women's preoccupation around food and body image when the domestic (the sustaining of daily life) was the only sphere of activity given to women, that same preoccupation imported to women's lives as they extend into the public sphere is monstrous. It is an outrage that we women should continue to bear this hallmark of oppression; that an enduring link between a private and public existence should be an obsessive concern with food and body image.

But you may well argue that food is a joyful matter. It is what nourishes us daily, it is an integral part of celebration, it is an act of community. Beauty, you may well argue, is a creative act. We dress to express ourselves, to play, to make statements. But alas this is rarely so unconflicted an activity for women. It is an area we do play in, but it is an area governed by constraints. This is not free play – adornment for pleasure, costume for temporary transformation, image for fleeting effect. It is far too serious for that. Far too meaningful. The image we manage to create still represents a relationship to self that evaluates acceptability from the outside; that looks for a place in society through what we can project rather than be; that depends upon seeing oneself as an object to be assessed rather than a subject with agency.

Sandra's collapse, a collapse bred of deep feelings of unentitlement to the food she gave others, to the care she gave others, to the life she nourished in others, is a marker of the continued distress women in the First World carry around food.

Food for women is so much more than the satisfaction of appetite and desire (indeed it is rarely that). Food is a language all of its own. Women have been denied not only a straightforward relationship to food, but a straightforward relationship to their emotional lives. Schooled to process emotions for others, they often have scant recognition of their own affective lives.

Indeed for Sandra and her friends, talking about food, dieting together, bingeing together, was part of social intercourse. Food talk became a way to say certain things to one another, and food became an internal communicator. They didn't say directly to another that they were unhappy, they said they were over-eating. They didn't dare acknowledge their fear, their hurt, their anger or the vast range of emotional responses to themselves. They ate instead and felt bad for over-eating or they didn't eat and felt temporarily good that they had avoided emotional pain. They shifted their emotional response to a manageable obsession; concern and guilt about food. But why should women – women who have taken on the task of managing emotions for the culture as a whole, be so fearful when it comes to their own that they have to be converted into the metalanguage of food?

With women's designation as domestic so went the designation of emotions. To put it in 1990s terms, as industrialized society privatized the family and women, so society privatized emotions. For the last two hundred years, the split between the public and domestic spheres has relegated women in general to the care of *others*, while denying women that care and attention themselves. Designated as possessions, as beauties, as wives, women have used their relationship to food and to the body to express the inexpressible of their experience. But the price of such expression is far too great.

On being invited to contribute to an anthology of food put together by Virago and Oxfam, I was struck by an awful irony. A women's-orientated publishing house and an aid agency collaborate on a project on food. But while we associate starving and malnutrition with societies in the Third World, we often daren't think of the voluntary starvation practised by women all over the West. On the face of it it seems crazy. Why should the general availability of food produce responses of guilt where a woman's desire is concerned? But it does. I hope I've given some pointers to why; to the desperately painful feelings besetting women and food.

I am not arguing for any equivalency here. Voluntary starvation and involuntary starvation or malnutrition are entirely different categories. Neither am I making a statement about the inevitable consequences of plenty. I'm simply making a plea for us to confront the distress surrounding the relationship of so many women to food.

The situation as regards women in the West *vis à vis* food is not inevitable. It flows from the social relations of a patriarchally-structured consumerist society in which women's sexuality serves the function of both humanizing the objects in the marketplace while becoming the ultimate object in themselves.

This is a tragic and horrific state of affairs. It is not a small problem but a vast social problem. It is a hidden suffering affecting literally millions of women. It involves many more women in the West than does alcoholism, than tranquillizer dependence and AIDS put together. And yet it is still trivialized. Laughed off. Denied or just simply taken for granted. It's time to put the problem of women and food on the agenda as a serious political issue.

Golden Chicken soup or Jewish penicillin – a mother's recipe.

Take a big pot. Clean 1 celery stick, 1 carrot, 1 medium onion. (Be careful not to use more, otherwise the soup will be too vegetably: 4 oz combined of carrot, celery and onion per 3 lb chicken is ample.) Put a cut-up hen (a boiling chicken) in the pot, add the vegetables, salt and white pepper, cover with water, bring it up to a boil, skim and turn it down to a slow simmer. Put a lid upsidedown on the pot. Fill the lid with water (so that liquid evaporates from the lid and not the soup) and leave it like so, topping up the water in the lid once or twice, for five hours. Drain. Put the soup in the fridge overnight. The next day or whenever you fancy, lift off the solid chicken fat that has risen to the top. Underneath you will find Golden Chicken soup. Serve to yourself when blue, ill, or in a celebratory mood.

You can use the chicken for chicken salad sandwiches. Or you can make second and third stocks as a base for other soups (use fresh vegetables, the same upsidedown-lid business).

Golden Chicken soup is traditionally served plain or with matzo meal dumplings (*knaidlech*), vermicelli (*lockshen*) or, if you want to go Italian, passatelli. All are delicious.

EDITOR'S NOTE

If possible, this should be made with a boiling chicken (hen): the flavour is better, and the bird doesn't go stringy with the long cooking. The small proportion of vegetables makes for a delicate aroma. this could be combined with Margaret Drabble's Lemon Chicken (page 64). For the non-kosher cook ordinary dumplings, or butter dumplings, rolled very small, could be added to the broth 15–20 minutes before serving.

Robyn Archer is Australian, an actor, author, singer and director. Now one of Australia's foremost entertainers, she has appeared live in Britain and on television. Based in Sydney, she lives, like most entertainers, out of a suitcase.

The Bigger Eat the Smaller

ROBYN ARCHER

THE stage is set for seascape.
Gulf Waters. Waves but not surf.
Incessant breaking on the shore.
A tyranny of tides.
Those who watch this scene must be aware
that these waves start in Antarctica,
and break quietly on these shores.

Immense fertility.
Dolphins swim up down the gulf,
close to the shoreline,
almost within reach of swimmers, who otherwise walk the beach
gazing up at the fortunate absolute beachfront houses,
neglecting to observe their willing playmates
who ride waves, and keep sharks at bay.

Two points away to the West
the great whites breed.
Their smaller brothers visit this beach
to chomp on the limbs and suck the blood of the unsuspecting.
All those childhood summers of
swim swim happy splash pre-cancer halcyon
suddenly the scream of siren
manually turned by brawny surfer, silly cap on head,
and little kiddies shrieking splashing harder
now and paddling fast, dog-paddling like some pooch
with crackers up its bum . . .

some tasty baby morsel for the predatory mouths
of eating machines in the

> FOOD CHAIN
> they hunt in packs
> these sharp-nosed punks
> and rap the reedy depths
> with 'CHAIN GANG' taunts and tunes
> to all the rest,
> the killer fish, that live to eat,
> The bigger eat the smaller

The beach is deserted
Enter a woman with a shipwrecked look.
Her clothes are torn and flimsy cotton,
into shreds that hang in ribbons
round her breasts which we can glimpse
and which are pretty, unexpected

She clutches a ham sandwich.
A fish cannot eat a pig.
Born in February she remembers,
and drops her sanger splat in sand.
It's not just sea salt stings her eyes, the tears have sprung
because she longed
to eat that pig in bread with deadly nightshade family fruit

Now it's unpalatable
smothered in the whitey grit
and stink of seaweed no one thinks to eat
they buy it in the Asian grocer
packed in Kyoto and costs a fortune
where we ship the cray from Kingston,
we can't buy it cheap no more,
where we ship the yabbies,
used to fish them with a hook and dead meat
up the creek don't do that now,
now export them, hard to get here anymore.

The seaweed's plentiful,
many-coloured, many textured,
yet they never think to eat it, only yell out
Poo mum stink,
ankle-biters who hate the slime, and skirt ten metres

round to keep away, next minute pick up fists of jelly-fish
the limpy lumpy ends of Man O'War
drifting in as clear gel playthings,
down the back of mum who's spreading Vegemite
on sandy-wiches for the kids, and now they'll get
'I'll give you such a belt, my girl'
and skidding off, go hungry, giggling
high and sweet against the wind . . .

the saltiness of tears springs thicker
'once I had three kids'
she wails
and contemplates the thing she can't eat,
hungry with remembering.
Once life was lived in untorn dresses
roof above the head, and little beds
for all the children.
What tidal wave of wasting, withering,
hurled itself against her shore
and left her like this, wailing
on an empty beach,
a hammy sandwich wedged between her toes
and only good for staring at amongst the haul
of starfish, sponge and broken shell
and tiny coloured whorls and clusters
stuck to razored mother-of-pearl?

When she can bear to raise her eyes
she feels the island to the South,
where sea-lions suckle while they sleep off
three days gorging out to sea.
The drag-net men destroy their larder
now they swim out fifty k, diving ever to the bottom
a thousand dives they make that way
to vacuum up the south sea bottom – prawns and crabs
crustaceans all, and then swim back and barely make it,
sees them dragging into shore,
sleeping where they dropped exhausted
no ounce left to find a bed.

Sleep it off, and burp and suckle,
make it to the dunes perhaps
maybe three days for collapsing

soon enough they're beckoned back.
Fifty k again they're swimming
Another thousand dives today,
how would humans go, no ounce of leisure?
'Lazy slugs' the tourists mutter
when they see the mammals spread

Sometimes, she thinks,
her life was like that.
Every ounce of nous consumed
in getting to the place for getting,
getting cash and hauling off to larders choc-a-bloc
with stuff – if you've got wherewithal consumption.
Haul it back to home, and stuff the kids
and fall asleep, and every time you've still not had enough
and up and on the street to start it over.

Her tears have dried

Enter a second woman.
The first still on her knees in abject worship
of the sandwich she has dropped,
observes the second, who is unaware . . .

She wears a silk sarong of gorgeous colours.
Some ethnic aboriginal print
of fishes, crabs, and crocodiles
in pointillistic primitive,
and colours like the tropic north,
of turquoise, cyclamen, and coral
bright new green comes out of fire,
her hair is clean, her legs are sturdy
barefoot on the sand she strides.
Head up, shoulders back, and rhythm in her walk
this one's got class –
cataloguing love and dinner, rich exotica of the past

She fills the stage with singing,
clear and passionate:

    The big fish in Mombasa, the candlelight, the mystery
    high above the harbour, bougainvillea round the terrace
    only two days drive from Tsavo,
    watching from the wooden terrace
    looking over the waterhole

elephants and tribes and babies
midnight herd, a thousand head of buffalo

The dusty whitened Lamu market
lobster bought and buttered, fried,
photographs of fruits and chillies
grating coconut on the roof
lengthy talks on prostitution
Gideon laughing fit to bust

Three-course dinner on the terrace
overlooking Lipari
Pasta fresca, marinara
insalata mista, Oscar, painter's wife, and twins and me
espressi heaven
half an inch of thickest black, makes you turn your back
on cities, specially in the midday heat
make no bones about the purest caffeine hit

Curried snails in Bangkok city
Got the trots in old Rangoon
Sat upon the front verandah
aglio olio by the light of the moon

This singing woman stops.
She looks down for the first time,
and sees this ragged other on her knees.
In bitterness the raggy one bites out
'Where the hell did you come from?'

The singing one replies;
'I was born seven miles from here,
and lived for twenty years among the dust and dry
Meat and three veg, Christmas pud and took a long old time
to see the other side.
I drank the milk of goats, and not from mother's breast,
and chicken wings were luxuries biennially.
Lots of bread and beans and bacon
camp pie, pumpkin, fritz and cheese.
Once I recall on dada's side, though, late at night,
around the poker table
the uncle hunter pulled out of his hessian sack
the wild duck he had shot and roasted whole
we snacked like Robin Hood and all his merry crew,

I might have even thrown a small bone over my shoulder
just to prove it.
And further up, around the port, we used to go
a-cockling and a-crabbing on the low-tide.
Funny to be back here – though I knew I would,
and you?'

The sandwichless castaway breaks her heart with crying
'I don't believe' she sobs
'you must be someone from the high side, happy . . .'

'Lower than a snake's arse'
the sheila-come-lately laughs, and waits, and softly says
'you look like you dropped your bundle'
observing the ham sanger almost buried at sea by now
'come up the house with me, I've got leftovers,
and I need breakfast. Coffee, I'll squeeze some orange juice.
You like spicey?
I've got an extra sarong too – and a few songs'

They leave together, walking away from the ocean,
turning their backs on sharks and dolphins alike
up the dunes
towards the fortunate beachfront house

Recipe for having a good time in the kitchen

Have a drink to sip – not like Hilary who would sip the sherry and wind
up under the table before the meal was cooked.
    Reserve heaps of time. Breathe easy.
    Put on some music.
    Sing and dance a bit while you prepare the food.

Songs by Me:

'Mettwurst Chewin' Momma' *The Ladies Choice* 1977
'Toots les Froots de Mer, Yeah!' *Ongoing Impro*
'Two Women Gazing at Each Other As If Their Lives Depended On It'
(title courtesy Lee Cataldi) has a breakfast verse
'Eating on the Plane' *Mrs Bottle* 1990
'Crazy Vegetables' *Mrs Bottle* 1990

Favourite Songs from the 1950s

'Coconut Woman' (Harry Belafonte)

'Jambalaya' (Hank Williams/Jo Stafford)
'Shrimp Boats Are a Comin'' (Jo Stafford)
'Come On a My House' (Rosemary Clooney)
'Crawdads' (Elvis Presley)
'Hey Good Lookin', Whatcha Got Cookin'' (Hank Williams)

Recipe from the Court of the Leftover Queen

cooking oil
onion
garlic
red chilli pepper
curry
garam masala (I dry heat seeds of coriander, cardamom, mustard, cumin, black pepper, grated nutmeg, until they pop, then pound them with mortar and pestle. See also p.146)
any leftovers from the night before (rice, vegetables, fruit, fish, meat, shellfish) or things before they go off in the fridge or the basket (capsicum, herbs – fresh coriander, basil)
fresh eggs

Cut the onion, garlic and capsicum (optional) yin-yang style, i.e., always downwards, not across in rings. Heat these and all spices (I just throw in whatever I reckon, depending on how hot I want it or which flavour I want to dominate) gently until the onion browns.

Add in any as yet uncooked vegetables or flesh and stir well into the spicy mixture.

Add a bit of filtered water to stop it sticking and a bit of salt if you eat it, which I scarcely do.

Heave in all the leftovers and stir them into the mixture. Add yoghurt (goat or cow) or coconut milk if you want it creamy, though this isn't advised if you want an egg on top.

Fry an egg.

EDITOR'S NOTE

This is one of those improvisations which depend on the inspiration of the cook and the ingredients to hand. In the trial cook-out, I added to the essential onions, garlic and seasonings, chicken from Susie Orbach's recipe (page 95), red pepper (capsicum) surplus to Elean Thomas's Curried Sheep Meat Stew (page 118), courgettes, rice left over from Attia Hosain's Khichdi *and* Kadhi *(page 21), and whole coriander seeds when frying the seasonings.*

DORIS LESSING

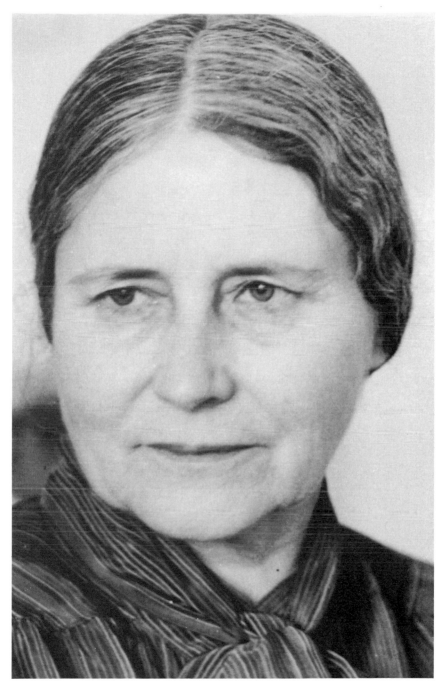

Doris Lessing was born of British parents in Persia, now Iran, and lived in what was then Southern Rhodesia for most of her early life. She has written non-fiction as well as her many acclaimed novels. She lives in London.

From: The Golden Notebook

DORIS LESSING

WHEN I get home the house is empty so I ring up Janet's friend's mother. Janet will be home at seven; she's finishing a game. Then I run the bath, and fill the bathroom with steam, and bathe, with pleasure, slowly. Afterwards I look at the black and white dress, and see that the collar is slightly grimy, so I can't wear it. It irritates me that I wasted that dress on the office. I dress again; this time wearing my striped gay trousers and my black velvet jacket; but I can hear Michael say: Why are you looking so boyish tonight, Anna? – so I'm careful to brush my hair so that it doesn't look boyish at all. I have all the fires on by now. I start two meals going: one for Janet. One for Michael and me. Janet at the moment has a craze for creamed spinach baked with eggs. And for baked apples. I have forgotten to buy brown sugar. I rush downstairs to the grocer's, just as the doors are closing. They let me in, good humouredly; and I find myself playing the game they enjoy: the three serving men in their white coats joke and humour me and call me love and duck. I am dear little Anna, a dear little girl. I rush upstairs again and now Molly has come in and Tommy is with her. They are arguing loudly so I pretend not to hear and go upstairs. Janet is there. She is animated, but cut off from me; she has been in the child's world at school, and then with her little friend in a child's world, and she doesn't want to come out of it. She says: 'Can I have supper in bed?' and I say, for form's sake: 'Oh, but you're lazy!' and she says: 'Yes, but I don't care.' She goes, without being told, to the bathroom and runs her bath. I hear her and Molly laughing and talking together down three flights of stairs. Molly, without an effort, becomes a child when with children. She is telling a nonsensical tale about some animals who took over a theatre and ran it, and no one noticed they weren't people. This story absorbs me so that I go to the landing to listen; on the landing below is Tommy, also listening, but with a bad-tempered critical look on his face – his mother never irritates him more than when with Janet, or another child. Janet is laughing and sploshing the water all around the bath, and I can hear the sound of water landing on the floor. In my turn, I am irritated, because now I shall have to wipe all this water up. Janet comes up, in her white dressing-gown and white pyjamas, already sleepy. I go down and wipe up the seas of water in the bathroom. When I return, Janet is in bed, her comics all around her. I bring in the tray with the baked dish of spinach and eggs and the baked apple with the clot of crumbly cream. Janet says, tell me a story. 'There was once a little girl called Janet,' I begin, and she smiles with pleasure. I tell how this little girl went to school on a rainy day, did lessons, played with the other children, quarrelled with her friend ... 'No, mummy, I didn't, that was yesterday. I *love* Marie for ever and ever.' So I changed the story so that Janet loves Marie for ever and ever. Janet eats dreamily, conveying her spoon back and forth to her mouth, listening while I create her day, give it form. I watch her, seeing Anna watch Janet. Next door the baby is crying. Again the feeling of continuity, of gay intimacy, starts, and I finish the story: 'And then Janet had a lovely supper of spinach and eggs and apples with cream and the baby next door cried a little, and then it stopped crying and went to sleep, and Janet cleaned her teeth and went to sleep.' I take the tray and Janet says: 'Do I have to clean my teeth?' 'Of course, it's in the story.' She slides her feet over the edge of the bed, into her slippers, goes like a sleep-walker to the basin, cleans her teeth, comes back. I turn off her fire and draw the curtains. Janet has an adult way of lying in bed before sleeping: on her back, her hands behind the back of her neck, staring at the softly moving curtains. It is raining again, hard. I hear the door at the bottom of the house shut: Molly has gone to her theatre. Janet hears it and says: 'When I grow up I'm going to be an actress.' Yesterday she said, a teacher. She says sleepily: 'Sing to me.' She shuts her eyes, and mumbles: 'Tonight I'm a baby. I'm a baby.' So I sing over and over again, while Janet listens for what known change I will use, for I have all kinds of variations in the words: 'Rockabye baby, in your warm bed, there are lovely new dreams coming into your head, you will dream, dream, all through the dark night and wake warm and safe with the morning light.' Often if Janet finds the words I've chosen don't fit her mood, she stops me and demands another variation; but tonight I've guessed right, and I sing it again and again and again, until I see she's asleep. She looks defenceless and tiny when she's asleep, and I have to check in myself a powerful impulse to protect her, to shut her away from possible harm. This evening it is more powerful than usual; but I know it is because I have my period and need to cling to somebody myself. I go out, shutting the door softly.

And now the cooking for Michael. I unroll the veal that I remembered to batter out flat this morning; and I roll the pieces in the yellow egg, and the crumbs. I baked crumbs yesterday, and they still smell fresh and dry, in spite of the dampness in the air. I slice mushrooms into cream. I have a pan full of bone-jelly in the ice-box, which I melt and season. And the extra apples I cooked when doing Janet's I scoop out of the still warm crackling skin, and sieve the pulp and mix it with thin vanilla'd cream, and beat it until it goes thick; and I pile the mixture back into the apple skins and set them to brown in the oven. All the kitchen is full of good cooking smells; and all at once I am happy, so happy I can feel the warmth of it through my whole body. Then there is a cold feeling in my stomach, and I think: Being happy is a lie, it's a habit of happiness from moments like these during the last four years. And the happiness vanishes, and I am desperately tired. With the tiredness comes guilt.

Elean Thomas, journalist, teacher, novelist and poet, was born in the Caribbean. She lived in London for some time, travelling widely to perform her poetry. She now lives in Jamaica.

Of National Dishes . . . Curried Goat or Curried Sheep?

ELEAN THOMAS

WE went into a Caribbean pub in the heart of Brixton, England. My white-Scottish-British-army-friend and I. He was the very one who took me to that particular Caribbean pub for the first time.

He had started going to that pub after the army authorities, whom he had served at home and all over the colonial world for nearly thirty years, declared him 'unfit for service' and threw him out of their army. People in the area told me that for years after that he had gone to that pub every evening and night and weekend . . . soon becoming every lunchtime and morning too. He kept inviting me for an after-work drink in the pub. I never had the time . . . too busy. Then he mentioned that it was not just any ole pub he was talking about. But a Caribbean pub. I sure found the time.

My white-Scottish-British-army-friend took me to share his refuge in a Caribbean pub in the heart of Brixton, England.

Because he liked the big, black, grinning African man who is the publican and who always welcomes him, even when often (as I was to learn later) my friend didn't even have a 50 pence to pay on his bill which was by then as long and winding as the River Nile. Certainly, one reason why the publican allowed my friend to run up such a long bill, is that he might have thought that, given the élite British regiment my friend had served in for almost all of his adult life, my friend must have been getting a fat army pension and disability benefits.

My white-Scottish-British-army-friend had had a tough time in those élite guards, being Scottish and all, instead of being English. But even those who didn't like him had to admit that he was among the best of military officers. And he would often boast about how the men of the subordinate ranks trembled when he called them to his office. From home, in Britain, he had been dispatched all over ... from Egypt to Kenya, from Malaysia to Singapore, from Germany to France. His final posting was Northern Ireland, from where he had to be retired, broken in body and mind.

After the more obvious of his wounds had mended and after he had learnt from the army authorities that he was not eligible for a special disability pension because those could only be given to war veterans, and Britain and Ireland were not 'in a state of war' when an opposition bomb reorganized his insides – after this, he started going to the Caribbean pub in the heart of Brixton, England.

My friend liked the fact that nobody there called him 'whitey'. Most of all, he liked the fact that nobody there knew he had been killing Africans. When evening after evening he would boast about his iron-disciplined-smart regiment, his own even smarter uniform, his military lick-and-spick exploits all over Africa and Asia, he never mentioned the line of small schoolchildren who had come singing across the bridge in Malaysia, just as he pressed the charge. Nor did he speak about the five young Kenyan men whom he personally tied up and burnt alive on the grounds that they were Mau Mau. He told me about them however. In one of the absolution-seeking sessions he used to try to have with me.

From Gus (was that really his name?) the publican, to Janet and Peter, the bartenders, to the group of retired London Underground men who still wanted Appleton white rum and Red Stripe beer, to the few fine-cured, iron-processed women whom any man disrespects at his peril, to the old, wizened Irish woman who hobbled around the pub picking up scraps of food from abandoned tables while getting her pint ... they all loved my white-Scottish-British-army-friend (or pretended they did). I was, on a later occasion, to see my friend cowering in abject silence in a corner of the pub when Gus's landlord of many years decided that he wanted to run the pub himself and came to evict Gus.

But my white-Scottish-British-army-friend loved the Caribbean pub because nobody there ever tried to make him feel as small as he knew he really was. So he felt confident to take his black-Caribbean-woman-writer-friend to his Caribbean pub in the heart of Brixton, England.

He stepped me into the warm and friendly noise of mixed peoples gathered. Ordered me a drink, then said to me, 'Choose from the menu anything that you may want.' Taking him at his word, my eyes noted but slipped past: CARIBBEAN-SEASONED CHICKEN. As far as I am concerned, chicken is acceptable prepared in any way, but, after all, chicken can be so boring, prepared in any way. I ran my eyes further down the menu board. They lighted on: BROWN-STEW LAMB CHOPS. Under normal circumstances, this would have been quite satisfactory ... yea, even welcome. However I was to go home to Jamaica within a week and I felt that if I abstained from sheep meat for a while, I wouldn't feel so bad the next time, some relative looked at me and said in utter disbelief: 'Yu mean to tell me dat yu eat SHEEP, girl! Lawd-a-massy!!'

In my ruminations, my eyes actually slipped past it, before they registered: CURRIED GOAT. I gave out a gasp of pure joy. My eyes began to flash like fire. I turned eagerly to my friend to let him know that I had made a definite choice.

In that moment, there appeared on the face of my white-Scottish-British-army-friend, a frown of deep and profound disappointment. A look of complete revulsion. And he ground out in a scornful voice, past the thin bars of his bloodless lips, 'You are surely not about to order that mess called CURRIED GOAT?!'

'Oh yes!' gushed I, unheeding, my mouth already filling up with waters of delicious anticipation of a tenderly-cooked, much peppered, plate of curried goat, boiled white rice and a soft finger of green bananas.

I saw and sensed his stomach retching. I began to feel very guilty. How could I be so insensitive to my friend as to fall down in worship of meat before a non-meat eater?

So I swallowed the mouth-juices awhile, till I could sound out the problem with my white-Scottish-British-army-friend. 'Are you a vegetarian or a vegan?', I asked my friend. Because he didn't answer right away, I continued, 'Please forgive me. I must apologize to you for bringing the notion of meat to our collective dining table.'

Said he; 'I am not a vegetarian or a vegan. In fact I do love my meat very much. I just cannot understand how an educated, civilized woman like you could even contemplate eating GOAT!'

Well, mi dear, I telling you the truth, dat one did floor me! Dat one did floor me right dung pon de linoleum inna di Caribbean pub inna di heart-a Brixton Inglan. Dat one floor me speechless. I tink dat some a di shot-dem weh im did fire pon de Kenyan-dem musta bounce-back inna im ead! Or him did drink mad puss milk! All dis time me jus-a look pon im like me cyaan believe it an im jus-a look pon me like im wan vomit. De people-dem inna de pub stop what dem was doing an-a look pon de two-a-we. Dem silent, silent, like dem-a expeck some crossroad. A fine back mi tongue at last and a sey to im:

'Oh! now, I understand. So perhaps I can help you my white-Scottish-British-army-friend, to also understand, if it is not already too late for you.'

Im a look pon me like me is duppy, transparent.

'I eat goat in the same way you eat sheep. Only that you never had many East Indians among you, so you don't have curry in your diet. I eat the stomach and intestines of animals in the same way you eat haggis. I call my dish "tripe and bean stew" and you call yours "haggis". I call my goat meat, "mutton". And you also call your sheep meat "mutton". You make a distinction between the meat of the baby sheep, which you call "lamb" and the meat of its mother or father, which you call "mutton". We don't. I eat goat. You eat sheep. We both eat "curried mutton" – you're not objecting to the curry, are you?'

Oh, no, no! He hastened to assure me.

'The goat and sheep are cousins. I love curried goat and you love curried sheep. We have a difference between us. But what does that difference matter to the goat and the sheep? They are both eaten by us.'

Gus gave out one of his belly-laughs. People went back to doing what they were doing before. My white-Scottish-British-army-friend is still looking dazed. I take his hand:

'Come, let us sit down together to eat what you call your supper and I call my dinner, in this Caribbean pub in the heart of Brixton, England. I won't criticize your haggis so long as you don't criticize my tripe-and-beans. I will leave your sheep alone so long as you leave my goat be.'

'Of National Dishes/Curried Goat or Curried Sheep' was inspired in Czechoslovakia and England (1984–1989); written in Maputo, Mozambique on 27 July 1989 and rewritten in Jamaica 1992 for *Loaves & Wishes*.

(For Wanjiru, Wanyiri and all the Kihoro family)

Curried goat or curried sheep
(Enough for 5 healthy eaters, 7 moderate eaters – gluttons could have it all in two eatings.)

1 lb goat meat or sheep meat, chopped into small pieces
2 lb rice (or any other starch if you're not a rice-eater)

Seasoning: (to your liking)
scallions (make sure you use the leaves, that's where the seasoning is)
2 small onions
salt to taste
1 level tsp curry powder (of course) shop-bought or homemade
natural pepper: the ones which grow green, red and yellow, on trees
(quantity to your liking but must be tasted in the completed dish)
garlic and herbs, including thyme, etc. as you like it

Vegetables: Irish potatoes, carrots, etc., as you like, keep in mind that the more vegetables you put in the more seasoning you have to put in.

Beware of turnips and other vegetables with too sharp a taste as they will conflict with the flavour of the curry sauce. Potatoes and carrots are ideal, since they allow the stew to 'stretch' to those two friends or relatives who just dropped by, at the same time that they make a rich gravy.

Season (marinate) the cut-up meat with curry powder and salt in a bowl or pot. If meat is dry, tip a little water in to moisten it up.

Add all the other seasonings and herbs, dicing, cutting-up, pounding or grating as necessary. Then add the potatoes and other vegetables. Leave to soak for at least half an hour. When you are ready to start cooking the meat, remove the vegetables from the same bowl/pot as the meat and seasoning.

Put your fire on a low flame. Put on the pot in which you are going to cook the curry. Tip just a little margarine/butter/cooking oil/or plain water into the pot. When it is reasonably heated, put in about a quarter of a teaspoon of curry. Beware of using too much curry powder, either in the seasoning or in the pot; your sauce could end up bitterish.

Give it a little time to fry or boil. Then put the seasoned meat into the pot. Cover the pot.

The heavier the pot, the better. All you now need to do is ensure that your flame is suitable for steaming for a half hour to forty-five minutes without burning. You can then go off and do whatever you do or yearn to do when you are not standing over the stove, so long as you keep peeking at the meat from time to time and keep stirring it around before it threatens to stick to the bottom of the pot. If it is getting too dry, tip a little water in, enough to ensure that you keep building up the liquid for the sauce.

When the meat is almost cooked, put in the vegetables, stir and cover to steam again for about another fifteen minutes (depending on how cooked you want the vegetables). If you overcook the meat or the vegetables, you will in fact end up with a 'mess' – a tasty mess . . . but a mess nonetheless. You want your curry sauce rich and plenty with bits of tender (not mashed) meat and vegetables almost floating in it, in whole pieces (mmmm . . . yummy . . . yummy . . .)

Within an hour from the time you started cooking, during which time you would have boiled the rice/potatoes, baked a cornbread, prepared a plain tomato or green salad, or just warmed/sliced-up some bread, your curried goat or curried sheep will be ready to eat. Enjoy it.

EDITOR'S NOTE

Like Maeve Binchy's Irish Stew (page 7) this is a traditional one-pot dish. The ingredients and their proportions can be varied according to the state of the household finances and the number of people who need feeding. British curry-powder must be more self-effacing than the Caribbean variety, as the quantity given imparts only a mild flavour. A good addition would be ladies' fingers (gumbo, okra) which give a satiny texture to the finished dish.

Sara Maitland was brought up in Scotland. She is a novelist and short-story writer, and has also written a book about women and Christianity, and a biography of the music hall artist, Vesta Tilley. She lives in London's East End.

Mother Love

SARA MAITLAND

I HATE to cook.

Of all the obligations that come with motherhood, the daily chore of feeding my household is the one I find most irksome.

It was not always so: there were dawns as pale as scrambled egg, when enthroned in pillows and delight, I fed my beautiful babies joyfully with food that I myself with diligence and love had prepared perfectly. The baby, who was hungry, would ask incessantly, determinedly for food. My grown-up self, dragged from crumpled dreams would protest strongly, resentfully; but my breasts would sing and full of milk would drip; white, delicately blue-veined, smooth and rich like dolcelatte *('sweet milk') cheese. Soft with sleep, wet with milk, the soft wet baby and I would be joined in the meal of paradise.*

Once upon a time, and not that long ago or that far away, 'I hate to cook' was practically a credal statement for feminists. We were *supposed* to hate to cook. The kitchen was our Gulag whither we were banished from the real world, and forced into slave labour; it was the symbol of our oppression, the focus of our discontent. We all hated to cook.

And then there was a sea-change; as gentle as dawn, quiet as an incoming tide, pine tables, homemade bread, shining Agas and candles at dinner drifted into our lives and, with them, wonderful food and decent wine. Alleluia. For do not get me wrong, I love food, I love to eat and drink, I love to be fed by my friends, I even love to entertain: to feed people, to have them eat and enjoy my food. I too have a large sunny kitchen, cheerful but sophisticated in greens and reds, and a long pine table and candles also and excellent coffee.

But obdurately, sullenly, I still hate to cook.

What I hate most of all is the daily feeding, nourishing, nurturing, cooking, of family life. I hate the constant attention that it requires; I hate the endless administration. I hate the repetitious decision-making, 'what will we eat today?' based on a demanding but profoundly uninteresting set of criteria: expense, vague outlines of good nutrition, willingness-to-consume, availability, time. The actual cooking can be fobbed off on others – all my family can and do cook meals – but the responsibility seems unshiftable. At least once a day there has to be a meal that everyone will eat. In addition there has to be a house full of things to fill in the gaps created by my own uninterest. And I hate the whole process.

The baby's sucking, or even – once feeding is established – the baby's crying, releases the hormone oxytocin into the mother's blood stream. Oxytocin helps the uterus to contract after childbirth and also triggers the 'let down' response, so that the maternal milk, stored deep in the breast in tiny sacs called the alveoli, flows down the milk ducts and into the ampullae immediately within the areola, the darker tissue surrounding the nipple itself. The rhythmic pressure of the baby's mouth on the areola, combined with the strong suction exerted by the child's tongue and throat draw the milk out of the breast and into the baby's stomach.

I do not entirely understand the source of this irritation with cooking. It is odd because I dote on my children and desire their well being, their nourishment and their growth. It is odd because I profoundly believe that eating together is one of the most important bonding mechanisms that we have. Little though I like having to organize them, prepare and present them, I still believe in family meals; my heart is still warmed, I am reassured, confirmed, by the sight of my family, and my friends, sitting round my table and eating my food. It is one of the central images of the folk stories I was brought up on; of the religion that I practise, and of my own childhood. In my parents' house meals were regular, delicious and warm. Breakfast, lunch, tea and supper followed each other ritually and smoothly; we were gathered there, rather than anywhere else, as family and our identity as family was strengthened in our shared activity of eating.

The process of lactation is true magic. No conjurer's razzmatazz and hocus-pocus. No fair Doreen, the passive lady helper, in glittered tights to bedazzle, distract and congratulate. Breast feeding is deep magic, deep contentment. 'Our duty and our joy' where the two cannot be separated. No one knows exactly how the relationship between the mother's chemistry, the child's desire, the mother's emotional gratification and the child's mechanical skills works, but it does work. The mother's body

*makes exactly the amount of milk that the baby needs or wants. There is
no wastage. There is simply milk: there when required, warmed to the
right temperature, immaculately sterilized, perfectly balanced nutrition –
although it looks pale and thin compared to cow's milk – low in sodium,
high in vitamins and calcium, lacking only iron which the neo-natal
baby does not need. The original fast food, that isn't junk food.*

*This is the old magic that Paracelsus burned his books to learn and
could not.*

My resentment about cooking is further odd, because actually, secretly, I
can cook – it is not the daily exposure of incompetence and inadequacy that
riles and humiliates me. It is touch and go sometimes, I admit, with my food,
but that is because I don't concentrate, not because I can't do it.

I was brought up to cook. My mother is, without question, the best
domestic cook I have ever come across. Food – solid, real, delicious,
thought-about food – comes out of her kitchen, out of her hands in a
never-ending flow of gastronomic pleasure. She is not a fancy foody cook,
but a real one. Abundance, that beautiful biblical concept, is the word for
her cuisine. Neither extravagance nor fuss, but excellence. 'Plain English
cooking' is usually a euphemism for bad, boring cooking: my mother's
kitchen transforms that term. I emerged from my childhood with all the
skills that that sort of labour-intensive culinary style teaches you. I have a
wooden spoon with a right-angled corner for scraping in the scratchy bits
from the roasting pan for gravy. I do not need to measure or weigh the flour
into a white sauce. I know what 'cook until done' means. I know you don't
have to be scared of soufflés – thermostats in ovens have changed all that. I
know that a little bit of very finely-diced carrot (or equally finely-diced liver
if you happen to have any lying around) makes all the difference to
bolognese sauce, and that macaroni cheese always tastes better reheated. I
know that flouring your apples makes the batter stick to them for fritters;
and, indeed, that the batter mixture is improved by standing. I know that the
secret of good meat is to chat up your butcher and the secret of good
vegetables is to grow them yourself. I have all this knowledge and no joy of
it. I watch my son, in my house a picky eater if ever there was one, digging
into his grandmother's food with an enthusiasm that staggers me, and I
don't even feel jealous. Both my sisters 'got it' somewhere along the line so I
can't even pretend that at some sub-conscious level my mother wanted to
keep this magical power to herself and deprived us subtly of her creative joy
in the task. It is very odd.

*There is a universality and a rootedness in the nursing of babies. Across
time, across continents, there is a sameness and a sisterhood. There is a
knowledge of both tiredness and tenderness that binds us together, we*

women who have nursed babies. I think perhaps this is why all the pictures, through all the Christian centuries, of the Madonna – whether she is queen of heaven or peasant girl – nursing the Holy Child, have an authority, a capacity to move, to touch the observer that is quite lacking in the anachronistic and gauche depictions of the childhood and infancy of Jesus. I think perhaps this is why I feel so strongly about the Nestlé's boycott: apart from the dangers into which small babies are being driven by formula feeding in societies where sterilization is hard to achieve, there are also the mothers being cut off from me, from this universal and transhistorical magic, from this absolute claim to power, stolen from them for profit by pointless technology. Perhaps this is sentimental. Nonetheless it is true.

So, I ask myself, what is the difference? No one can say that cooking is as demanding, as tiring, as repetitive, as constant and as unalienable as breast feeding. Why then did I find breast feeding such a pure joy and cooking such an impure burden. I have no brief for the glories of biologically ordained femininity.

Perhaps it is the immediacy: there is a hungry baby, here is the food it wants, the food produced in, and only in, response to its hunger. It does not want it in a hour or so: it wants it now. There is no gap between the desire and its fulfilment. The baby does not say on Thursday that it would like packed lunch tomorrow; and can we eat early the next day? There is nothing to plan; nothing to think about in advance.

Perhaps it is the physicality of it: the nakedness and the range of extraordinary sensations, from the heavy flowing outward of the milk to the slightly ticklish tweakings and mumblings of a contented playful child. I am told about the sensuality of cooking; the smells, the tastes, the rich variety. I acknowledge the sensual experience of burned fingers and over-salted potatoes, but neither meet the delineations of my desire.

Perhaps it is the expectation aroused by cooking: neither of my babies ever turned to me in the night when I brought them my body and said – 'yuck!' or 'boring'. No one asked about 'balanced nutrition'. There was no way I could do it better (or worse) than any other woman; there was no way I could do it worse (or better) than any man. I did not even have to absent myself from competition: there was no competition. Breast feeding takes up the time it takes: there are no short-cuts, no clever dodges, no feeling that if you gave it more thought, more effort, more concentration there would be any conspicuous improvement.

Perhaps it was just the first thing I did for each of my children. It had novelty value, and it did not go on for very long. I breast fed them for a total of twenty months; I shall be cooking for them for well over twenty years.

Perhaps it was the one-to-one intimacy of it, like love making. It was for no one else; there was no balancing of needs, just the meeting of them in a direct but somehow secret way; a secrecy, an intimacy that remained even when the actual feeding was done in public.

Perhaps it is the social construction of cooking as 'women's work'. The relationship between breast feeding and being female is very simple, and inescapable. I felt no real resentment against my husband for not doing it. I do feel 'put upon' by his, and the children's expectations about food. What goodwill they might generate, and what firmness I might exercise, is constantly undermined by a world out there which will insist they do their duty and construct their mother as loving by making her take on this task.

Perhaps I'm a slut and a bad mother.

Perhaps I'm a breast fetishist with no better way to express my narcissistic self-adoration.

I don't know.

I do know that I love them now, and want to nurture them and have them grow and be well. I would have liked to have been able to carry the strong and positive feelings I had about the bond of food when they were tiny into a more grown-up but equally enchanting bondage as they worked their way towards adulthood. But I move into middle-age with the joyful realization that that sort of cooking will soon be over, and also the shadowy sorrow that never again will I feed a child at my breast.

Recipe

My children, collapsed in laughter that anyone should ask me for a recipe, offered the following:

Family Supper *à la maison Maitland*

Ingredients: see method.

Method: Decide to have spaghetti bolognese. Slice onion, while grumbling. Fry onion, add meat to pan. Discover there are no tomatoes. Swear. Pour large gin. Wrap up meat-and-onion mixture and place in freezer (still hot). Find elderly pizzas in freezer. Place under grill. Throw gin away mistaking it for water. Swear. Pour second large gin. Answer phone and talk with great animation to friend. Notice clouds of smoke from grill. Swear. Pour third large gin. Send someone to chippy. Discover there is no vinegar. Insist everyone eats fish-and-chips without vinegar, except self. Pour fourth large gin.

This is unfair. Here is a very good quick recipe for spaghetti. Among its other advantages, children hate it!

pasta
small onion
clove garlic
2 to 4 bacon rashers
butter
½ lb chicken livers
oregano
single cream
(vary the amounts of pasta and cream according to how many people you
want this to feed: 2 to 4 is reasonable)

Put the pasta on to boil.

While it is cooking, finely chop onion and crush garlic and chop bacon;
fry them all gently in butter; add chicken livers chopped up (with nastier
bits snipped out with scissors) continue frying. The chicken livers will
break up if you stir hard, and prod a bit: this is to be encouraged. Add
oregano, salt and pepper.

This takes about as long as the pasta takes to boil.

Drain the pasta. Stir the cream into the chicken liver sludge. Heat but
don't boil. Pour it over the pasta. Stir well. Serve with salad.

EDITOR'S NOTE
*You will need quite a lot of cream if this is for guests, and plenty of
freshly-ground black pepper.*

Marina Warner is British, with an Italian mother. As well as being a distinguished critic and historian, she is an acclaimed novelist and has written a libretto for a children's opera. She lives in London.

The First Time

MARINA WARNER

THE serpent had decided to diversify; the market economy demanded it. Jeans, soft drinks, bicycles and sunglasses had learnt to present themselves in subtly different guises; so could he.

So he took a training course in nutrition. In his first job (for he showed talent), he was issued with an instantly printed label identifying him as 'Lola – Trainee Customer Service Assistant', and he wangled himself a pitch on the Tropical Fruit Stand in the Tropical Fruit Promotion that was taking place in order to add a little cheer to the London winter.

To attract the customers' attention, the serpent called Lola was togged up in tropical costume and put on his warmest mother-hen voice. There were OAPs with plastic shopping bags on wheels and hair in their noses; they tasted the little cubes of fragrant juicy this and that which Lola had cut up and flagged with their proper name and country of origin, but one said he would think about it, dear, and another made a face and said the stringy bits were too stringy. Lola wasn't sure the game was worth the candle in their case. She was after brighter prizes. The serpent in her liked fresh material; a challenge. And Pity, it turned out after all, was not unknown to him.

Then Lola spotted a customer, a likely lass, a young one made just as she fancied, quite ready for pleasure, pleasure of every sort, a hard green bright slip of a girl, barely planted but taking root, and she held out in her direction one of the nifty transparent plastic cups like a nurse's for measuring out dosages in hospital, with one of the tasty morsels tooth-picked and flagged inside it, and she urged her to eat. (She was speaking aloud in one voice everyone could hear, and under her breath in another that she hoped her young shopper would listen to, secretly. This was a trick the serpent had perfected over centuries of practice.)

131

'Come here, my little girly, I have just the thing for a cold day, bring some sunshine back into your life.

(I know what it's like, it's written all over you. He fucked you to death three days ago – oh, is it a whole week? – and you haven't heard from him since. Your face is pale, your brow is wan and you can't understand what you did wrong. Well, you can tell me all about it)

'There's nothing Lola, your Trainee Customer Service Assistant, can't provide. It's Tropical Fruit Week – just move over this way – we have passion fruit and pawpaw (that's payaya by another name) and prickly pear and pitahaya and guava and tamarillo and physalis and grenadillo. Not to mention passion fruit. Each one has been flown here from the lands of milk and honey where they grow naturally, as in the original garden of paradise, and they're full of just that milk and honey, I'm telling you, you can hear the palm trees bending in the breeze on the beach and the surf breaking in creamy froth on the sand and they reach the parts other things don't reach

(the tingly bits, the melting bits and rushes-to-the head and the rushes to places elsewhere than the head – well I shan't go on, but your troubles are at an end if you just come a little bit closer, so I can pick up the signals in your dear little fluttering heart, my sweet, and whisper in your ear)

'As I say it's Tropical Fruit Week and this is the Tropical Fruit Stand! With a dozen different varieties of fruit from all over the world, many new, exciting and delicious flavours for you to sample, and

(let me add this under my breath so only you can hear – they all have different powers, they can work wonders in all kinds of different ways – they're guaranteed to fix up your little problems before you can snap your fingers and say What the hell, and what the hell, I know all about that, I know the hell you're in, believe me. And I also know how to stop it hurting)

'I know because I'm fresh from the Healthy Eating consultancy course in our company headquarters in Stanton St James, Gloucestershire. We were given an intense fortnight of nutritional experience, and there's nothing I can't tell you now about fruit –'

And the serpent, to his great joy, saw that the young girl was getting interested, and coming closer, with her shopping list crumpled under one hand on the bar of the supermarket trolley and the other twiddling a strand of her hair near her chin, as she came closer and looked at Lola's spread of little plastic cups with pieces of fruit in each one. She was so close that Lola could hear her thinking

132

i was all clenched up cos i was scared it's not everyday i do it you know in fact i don't do it very often though looking at me you might think so and i like to make out i'm a one cos otherwise you look a bit of a wimp don't you i mean everyone else is doing it, aren't they? and my mother said keep smiling the men don't like scenes they don't like glooms if you want to drive a man away just keep that look on your face and the wind'll change men don't like a woman all down in the dumps who'd want to spend a minute with you it'd be like passing the time of day with a ghoul

And Lola took charge of the situation, it was her job to bring a little sunshine back into winter; pleasure was her speciality. So she began, 'Take mango for instance, now the instructions say, "Make sure the rind is rosy-yellow and slightly yielding to the touch – green mangoes are inedible." Just like it says there, on the label, a mango, when it's properly ripe and ready, is full and juicy and its sweetness runs all over your hands and gives off this deep rich scent –

(I don't have to go on, do I? A good man is going to know that and if he don't know it, he's no good and you can drop him, my sweet and find another one who understands these things. The first thing you must get into your little head, sweetheart, is that if you were clenched up like you said it wasn't anybody's fault but his)

i tried to be lighthearted and cheerful while it was going on but it kept getting to me all the same and making me sad, sex does that to you it lifts you up but it doesn't last it drops you down again from a great height and now i can't concentrate on anything cos i keep seeing him doing things to me and doing them back i was trying to keep a brave face on it but i know i was disappointing not passionate like he knows it from other girls it wasn't new to him like it was to me he knows that i could sense it but i don't like the neighbours to hear anything cos when they're at it and i hear and mum is out and i'm alone it makes me feel funny.

'Take this guava, for instance, it's in perfect condition. Sometimes when you pierce one of these fruits, they're not quite ripe yet. You have to wait for the ones that aren't ready, you can't rush them. But the ones that are over-ripe, gone soft and spongy, you have to throw those away . . .

(don't you worry any more, my little girly, you'll be fine. You're just lacking confidence, that's all it is, and you wanted to please him, when really you should just think how much pleasure there's in it for you. Never forget that, it's the first rule. My sweet little girly, you're a perfect little girly and he's a fool if I know men – and I do – forget him and find another one who'll appreciate you)

it's a bit shocking, really, i didn't expect such a mess, both of us leaking this and that, i did melt at first, stickiness afterwards he seemed to like it, he held on to me tight, he asked me if i cared for him and i said i did, and his heart was thumping and it seemed like a promise it was a promise, it must have been some kind of a promise . . . but then nothing not another sight of him not a word what did i do wrong what can i do now

(when he comes back and he will you know, he'll be round with his tongue hanging out, you must be ready, so come closer still – you are a sweet and tender pretty little girl, aren't you, yum yum, no wonder he liked you, he's probably just frightened of coming back because your hold on him's too strong, believe me, I know. You're at just that dangerous age, and your hair smells good, vanilla and grass and peach and a trace of sweat, that's good, very good –

The young girl's head was very near Lola now, as she bent over the little measuring cups with their pink and yellow and crimson offerings, sniffing at this one and that one, daring, daring to taste one.

'Peaches don't count as tropical, but they have restorative powers too, I'm telling you, and now we can grow them all the year round, that's the wonder of modern agronomy – agronomy – the science of growing foods

(anyhow, darling, just any one of these tropical fruits will give him what he wants from you and then you'll have him in the palm of your hand. Try slipping him a fat cactus fruit, with the spines cut off, mind – or if you're ambitious, try pawpaw – papaya by another name as I was saying and it's no accident that this is papa-fare, ha ha. It's a fruit for daddy's girls, firm and slippery)

'and its juice makes an excellent meat tenderizer if you want to add it to a marinade or you can just open it and eat it all, yes, seeds and all. Or there's tamarillo here, it's full of rich pulp under the tight shiny skin and the flavour's sweet and sour when it's ripe, and has many culinary uses, in desserts as well as savoury dishes . . . Eat it when the skin's turned a deep red, and the fruit's firm but yielding to gentle pressure . . .'

(that's right, you start giggling, you'll be fine even if it's all over with him there'll soon be another one – I'm telling you, Live for passion, there's nothing better and that's the second rule and all men and women are fools who don't grasp it)

it began like that he said, trust me, and then you open up first your mouth and his mouth and then, well . . . sometimes i envy men, they know what other women are like, i wonder if i'm like his other ones, he must have had lots, he felt like he knew what he was doing. i was a bit scared, he's older than me just two years but it makes a difference and he's got a reputation at school, that's what made me interested in the first place so i bit down on my fears, other girls do it all the time, i must get on with mum's shopping it might give that assistant ideas, my hanging around here maybe i should try one of her fruits she looks silly standing there in that tropical outfit with the headcloth and the fruit earrings dangling and the bangles over her surgical gloves, she's using a little sharp knife, with these funny knobbly and lumpy fruits she's egging on to customers, the OAPs with their shopping bags on wheels and their nose-hair sprouting, so now it's my turn and i point to one of the little plastic cups with the fruit inside on a toothpick and she's saying to me,

'Go on, try, you're under no obligation to purchase – I don't even have the fruits here on my stand, you have to go to the fruit and veg section and choose your own. We're here to educate the public, to raise the standards of nutrition and health in the households of this country, especially where there are children and young people, growing up

(like you, my dear, so silky and soft and lovely with just that whiff of unwashed . . .)

'There's pitahaya for you too – firm as a pear and slightly perfumed, like rose petals – it's refreshing! Here, you can eat it like a dessert fruit, you peel it like this, lengthways, the rind comes off smoothly, it's related to the prickly pear, but this one hasn't got any prickles. Or you can slice it into salads – add a dash of colour to your salad bowl, keep the winter at bay with Tropical Fruit from the parts of the world where frost can't reach and the sun always shines, scoop out the pink flesh and taste the sunshine!'

we didn't use anything it seemed mean to ask him to as if i thought he was diseased or something so now i don't know i could be pregnant – are you happy to be pregnant the ads ask? – i could be i suppose – i can feel something inside me it's like a letter Y it's either a sperm wriggling or it's one of the those cells they go on about on the telly reproducing itself all wrong and giving me aids

(now that was silly, very silly, you can't have the pleasure that's due to you, my girl, if you're careless, that's the third rule. But if you bend your ear I'll let you in on the way to have fun – never do that again, this time you'll be all right, I can tell, I can see and hear things other people can't and –)

'there's nothing like fresh fruit to build up your immune system, clean out your insides, keep you healthy and lean and full of energy

(as I say, you're in luck this time but don't try on anything like that again)

'in these days of pollution and other problems – I mean we've all wised

135

up to the devastation of the rainforests and their connection to . . . well, I shan't talk about meat-eating because we still have a butcher's counter here – all free range, of course – but anyway what with acid rain and the hole in the ozone layer and the thinning of the oxygen supply and the little creepy crawly things out of the tap in your water – you need Fruit! Fresh fruit goes straight to the immune system and kick starts it into a new life . . .'

Eventually the serpent was successful: his fresh, young, sad target dropped her mother's shopping list somewhere on the floor of the supermarket and forgot everything that was on it and came home instead with

    1 mango
    1 pitahaya
    2 pawpaws
    4 guavas
    2 tamarillos
    6 passion fruit
    and 13 p change

Her mother said, 'Where's the Brillo Pads, then? And the milk for you and your brother's breakfast tomorrow? Where's the bacon for tonight's supper? And the bread?'

Her daughter told her about Lola, about the Tropical Fruit Stand and Tropical Fruit Week. She kept quiet however about some of the other things that had transpired between her and the Sales Assistant.

Her mother scolded, her mother railed: 'In my day, an apple a day kept the doctor away – now you have to have . . .' she picked up the guavas and the soft but firm mango and the tubular and prickle-free pitahaya and smooth and slippery pawpaw. 'What do you do with this stuff anyway?'

'I've brought the leaflet – look!'

'Apples were good enough for us, and they should be good enough for you. And when I write down a pound of apples on the shopping list I mean a pound of apples, I don't mean any of this fancy rubbish. Your generation doesn't understand the meaning of no; you just believe in self, self, self, you want more, more, more. You think only of your own pleasure. You'll be the ruin of me. I don't know, I try to bring you up right . . .'

' "Plump and rounded or long and thin, it has a distinctive firmness of texture and delicacy of aroma . . ." ' she read, and she thought she heard her mother stifle a snort as she kept on with the Tropical Fruit Week Promotion package.

if he doesn't come back that lady was right i'll just find another one what she said made sense he thought he was something but was he anything to write home about anyhow i feel better about it already i'll go back to school and i'll just make out it meant nothing to me nothing and i don't care about him she was wicked she was strong i liked her

Lola was still at the stand, back in the shop, doing her patter, to other customers passing by.

'Guava, passion fruit, tamarillo! Let me just tell you exactly how you can put each one to good use –'

And meanwhile she was thinking,

(my little girly, you're young, you're inexperienced, but you'll soon know so much. You'll look back on this and you'll laugh or you won't even remember that you ever felt so pale and wan. In fact you might even look back and wish that you could feel something as sweet and real and true as this first-time pain you were feeling till I taught you the three principles of pleasure and set you on my famous primrose path)

Recipe
Take fresh fruit in season
Squeeze

Attia Hosain born in Lucknow, was the first woman graduate of her extended family. She moved to London in 1947, the year of Indian Independence (and partition). She is a journalist, broadcaster, novelist and short-story writer, and divides her time between London and India.

Of Memories and Meals

ATTIA HOSAIN

I CAME in the summer of 1947 to a London of dark streets, bombed buildings and very strict rationing. Outward forms did not matter to me; I was an explorer in a city I had always known in my mind.

Then, suddenly, a year earlier than expected, India became independent, but partitioned, with families divided. Ten million refugees were on the move, and a million died. I had to make a choice between two countries and chose a third – Britain with its centuries old historical ties.

The path to exile is paved with ideals, and the journey through loneliness to nostalgia begins.

I began to go more often to a restaurant called Shafi's because it was a rendezvous for Indians – visitors, expatriates and students alike. For all who came from a country where food and companionship went naturally together, Shafi's was like being back home. The owner was host, friend and confidant to all who came, whether to eat, or just to relax and talk.

Never in India had I found myself alone at any meal. It would have been unthinkable not to share food with friends and relatives. To break bread together has always been a token of friendship; to eat salt together is a symbol of loyalty.

In those early days away from home the loneliest were those celebrating festivals especially *Eid-ul Fitr*, the day Ramadan, the month of fasting, ended. It was always a family celebration, with relations and friends – all part of an extended family – coming with joyful greetings, regardless of religion or status. Everyone wore new clothes or something new if unable to afford them. The young were given a *rupee* as a token of blessing by their elders. A special sweet, *seviyan*, made of delicate vermicelli cooked in milk with

141

cardamoms, almonds, pistachios and sultanas decorated with silver leaf, was served to visitors and all members of the household.

Sweets were offered no matter what the occasion as a token of good wishes that life would be as sweet.

Later there was the *Eid*, which commemorated the willingness of Prophet Abraham to sacrifice his only son Ismaiel. After the sacrifice of sheep or goats the meat was distributed amongst friends, relations and most importantly, sent to orphanages and distributed to the poor. Some of it was reserved for the family and those who were part of the household staff. Naturally there was a surfeit thereafter of meat dishes, *kormas*, roasted legs of lamb, *biryanis* and *pulaos*, and many kinds of kebabs, all with a different taste and shape. I loved them more than the most elaborate dishes.

I can still recall a day all those long years ago when, far from home, a friend and I were walking along Oxford Street after a broadcast, having eaten a canteen meal of powdered eggs and wilting lettuce leaves. We were homesick for Lucknow, the city of our birth, but not for its beauty, its refinement, the sound of its poetic language or its culture. We talked longingly of food and of one in particular which was famous.

'Oh, for Toonda's kebabs!' we sighed. 'Oh, for a warm *chapati!*'

Nowhere else were *chapatis* as large, as light, as delicate.

Toonda, who made kebabs known to all connoisseurs of good food, was given that nickname because he had lost an arm up to his elbow and yet was a culinary artist. His kebabs were best eaten the moment they were ready and queues formed in front of his shabby shop by the old city gate. It was in the narrow street where *attar* [scent] makers, *chikan* [embroidery] sellers, the makers of gold and silver leaf which was used to decorate festive food and sweets, had had their shops since the days Kings had ruled in Lucknow.

The sound of music came from the balconies of houses overlooking the street where courtesans lived who had once taught etiquette to the aristocracy. Our nostalgia made everything a background for Toonda's kebabs.

Walking along dark London streets, I would recall *Diwali*, the festival of lights in honour of Lakshmi, the goddess of wealth, when streets were bright with revelry and every house was outlined with the glow of tiny oil lamps. Our home was lit to welcome our Hindu friends and wish them good fortune and prosperity. Small animal shapes made of sugar were sold in every sweet shop and were the best gifts for children.

During Christmas with nowhere to go, knowing it as a family festival, I remembered Christmas at home, visiting our friends, joining in their singing of carols, eating Christmas cake and mince pies, none as delicious as those made for us by our loving and loved Christian Ayah, Sally Peters, who shared all our festivals. So too did my Amma, my wet-nurse. When I was older she was put in charge of the kitchens. She supervised the storerooms in which stood jars which could have held Ali Baba's forty thieves. In those were stored the wheat and lentils and rice, the harvest of the fields, brought from our ancestral village by bullock carts with large wooden wheels. There were tins containing *ghee* [clarified butter] and mustard oil. There was a large grinding stone on which the corn and wheat were ground by women sitting on the floor of the storeroom's verandah. They made curds, buttermilk, *ghee* and clotted cream from the milk of cows which lived by the stables.

In a smaller storeroom there were fragrant bottles of *keora* [kandanus extract] and rose-water, tins of sugar and spices, and baskets of onions, garlic and herbs.

When special delicacies and seasonal sweets and *halvas* were to be prepared, Amma saw to it that everything was ready in the courtyard by the lawn and garden of the *zenana*. Two or three string-woven beds with carved legs, covered with colourful *durries*, were brought out, and low stools, and large coal-burning braziers on which to cook. My mother, my sisters, my aunts and cousins would join in the preparation and the cooking, helped by the maids. There would be a fragrance in the air and the sounds of voices laughing and gossiping.

I was reprimanded because I would not join in the cooking as other girls did. I hated cooking because it stole time from my books, but I liked good food and I did not have to cook it then.

But necessity is a hard teacher. In London, as a single parent with two young children, I had to learn to cook. I even wrote a cookery book thirty years ago. One had to make do then without spice shops round every corner. I learned to cut corners and save precious time.

When I remember the past I still wonder how the most elaborate feasts were prepared for hundreds of guests. There were no sophisticated, automated, complicated, mechanically perfected cookers, grinders, blenders, steamers, timers, gas and electricity, just brick and clay stoves, and coal and wood to burn, and heat regulated by how much was used or removed.

Cooks were not just craftsmen but artists. They knew exactly which spices in what quantities were used with each kind and variety of food. Specialist cooks – often for one particular dish – were rivals, and vied with each other in producing dishes perfected in their delicacy and subtlety of taste and aroma. They kept their recipes secret, handing them down from father to son. Accurate measurements were discarded; long years of apprenticeship and practice, and sensitive senses of taste and smell were their guides. 'A pinch of this, a pinch of that, fistfuls of rice, fistfuls of lentils, water measured to the joints of a finger or thumb'. '*Andaz sé*' [approximately] was the answer to questions about measurements. Experience was their teacher.

Each season had its own kind of food, and all spices were used according to whether they were heating or cooling; and always in relation not only to taste but their essential preservative and medicinal qualities. It was part of religious belief to distribute portions of food amongst the poor, whether it was cooked for joyous occasions or to commemorate deaths. Fundamentally nothing has changed.

The older one is the more vivid are the memories of youth that are part of a tale once told. I remember the songs, devotional or festive, sung by the young girls and women, particularly during the season of the rains. A fragrance rose from the dry earth when the first rains fell, and the fields became green, and the farmers knew that their crops would not wither and would bear fruit. I think specially of the mangoes known as *Samar Behisht*, the 'Fruit of Heaven', about which we were told 'Eat the fruit when it wants to be eaten, not when you want to eat it'.

When living in our ancestral village home we walked along green and gold fields, and from the sugar-cane fields we cut pieces to chew and savour the fresh juice. From that juice was made the *gur* [jaggery] that sweetened the green mangoes cooked with semolina, a much-loved summer favourite, as were the cooling sherbets made from fruits or nuts. Even the street cries of hawkers we heard in Lucknow were poetic. I still recall one: 'I sell the fingers of Laila, the ribs of Majnoon'. (Laila and Majnoon were tragic lovers in a classical Persian poem. Majnoon starved to death for unrequited love.) All that was being sold was a delicate variety of cucumbers!

It is the use of spices which characterizes Eastern food, and it was spices that changed the history of India. For thousands of years traders had sailed to and from India for the gold, precious stones, silks and cottons of that rich country, and spices, too. Then three hundred years ago a new kind of trader arrived. They came to trade; they stayed to rule.

When Sir Thomas Roe came as Ambassador from England to the splendid court of the Mughal Emperor Jehangir and gained his favour, he was allowed to establish a trading post and fortify and garrison it. What Sir Thomas had started, but with fewer trading subterfuges and larger garrisons, was continued by men like Robert Clive, and India was finally acquired as 'The Jewel in the Crown'.

A country had lost its freedom for peppercorns.

For us food has many connotations beyond nourishment, mostly sacramental, often part of history. I remember my grandmother telling me stories of the 'Mutiny' of 1857. *Chapatis* were sent secretly from village to village as a signal for revolt against the British. Years later Mahatma Gandhi used fasting as a non-violent weapon against their rule and every one of us felt involved. I grew up in a home where there was little gossip and much political talk when the family and friends gathered around the table for meals.

Years of living in the West have made me increasingly conscious of the differences between our attitudes to food. Even the poorest of Indians will never turn away an unexpected visitor at mealtimes, and will say 'Share my *dal roti*', their staple and sometimes only food.

I understand why this cannot happen in Western homes: it is because of the kind of food generally cooked, in measured quantities for each individual. There is also a barricade of rules and etiquette. Spontaneity must remain a word unknown.

I have always found such rules constricting. Our family meals reflected the duality of our lives, the merging and clash of two cultures. There was always one *Angrezi* [English] dish, together with the traditional food. And when there were English guests the correctly English five courses were served, together with an elaborate *pulao* and its accompaniments. I preferred the simplicity of the traditional ways, without the paraphernalia of heavy cutlery and crystal and the orders of precedence.

Sometimes I am asked by well-meaning people concerned about the world, often after a lunch or dinner watching distressing pictures of starving children of the Third World, 'How can one bear to live surrounded by so much poverty and starvation?'

How does one answer? Should one say, 'How does one live in a world where food is destroyed and farmers are subsidized not to grow it because of market forces? How can one use food as a bribe or withhold it from the starving except when riots and revolutions endanger economies?'

Should I ask what one can do with the 500 million human beings who live below the poverty line amongst the 800 million in India? Say 'Vanish'? They cannot be hidden in the inner corners of cities or on reservations. They leave their villages when the rains fail, when crops die, when there are too many mouths to feed, and migrate to cities in search of work and food.

What are we who live in cities to do? Leave? Go where? We can do only whatever is humanly possible, by every means possible. We have witnessed their courage and the miraculous survival of their human dignity and spirit, and have learned humility and gratitude.

My wise old Ayah used to say 'An empty stomach cries out for an answer'. Today that cry is loud in the world.

I was taught from childhood of the sanctity of food. Not a piece of bread could be thrown away without kissing it and raising it to one's eyes as with all things holy. We were taught to say silently before each meal 'In the name of God'. At school I joined in saying Grace.

These are some memories and traditions I would never change or lose.

Dal

Dal (lentils) is a favourite food of mine, more than any gourmet dish, because it is simple to cook, very nutritious and inexpensive. I don't cook by the traditional method, and add all ingredients I think are healthy. I leave out oil or *ghee* myself, but they do add to the taste for anyone not strict about a fat-free diet.

Masoor Dal (orange lentils found in any grocery shop)

7 oz lentils

1½ pints water

2 cloves garlic, crushed well

1½ tsp ginger, finely chopped

1 large green chilli (optional)

1 tsp *garam masala*

½ small onion cut into thin circles

2½ tbs oil or *ghee* (clarified butter optional)

1 tsp cumin seeds

Keep all ingredients ready.

Wash lentils thoroughly. Soak for fifteen minutes. Drain and put in saucepan with 1½ pints water. Bring to the boil rapidly, turn down heat to simmer and skim off any scum on the surface.

Add the turmeric, garlic, ginger, onion, green chilli and salt and pepper to taste.

Stir well then simmer until the *dal* is soft, stirring occasionally to prevent sticking.

After half an hour the *dal* should be ready for the final steps before serving.

Stir in the *garam masala* and stir.

Heat the oil or *ghee* well in a small saucepan. Add the cumin seeds until they are dark brown. Add to the *dal*, and quickly cover the pan to preserve the flavour and aroma.

Serve with rice and any vegetable or meat dish.

Afterword: About Oxfam

ROBERT CORNFORD

Loaves and Wishes is a project that mirrors Oxfam in many ways. It links different countries of the world; it brings together women from the countries of the North and the South through a shared experience; it is a celebration of common humanity; and it engages contributors in an area of their expertise in support of Oxfam. It is also stimulating, questioning, argumentative, pointed and – we hope – will give pleasure to those who read the book.

Oxfam is particularly pleased to be associated with Virago in this project as it gives an opportunity for us to talk to a new constituency, and we hope that many readers will make a long-term engagement with Oxfam through *Loaves and Wishes*. The addresses of Oxfam offices around the world are at the end of 'About Oxfam': do contact us.

Working for a fairer world

In an age when space travel, the most potent symbol of technological progress, is commonplace you might think that poverty on earth is a thing of the past. You would be wrong.

Every day, millions of people in the countries of the South go without things we in the developed countries of the North take for granted: food, shelter, water, education, health care, and the right to make decisions about our own lives.

In fact, for many poor people things are getting worse, not better.

Oxfam is helping people break out of their poverty by supporting them in their efforts to make changes that will last. Oxfam has been doing this in different ways around the world since 1942.

The early years

In 1942 the world is at war. Most of Europe is occupied by Nazi forces, and innocent civilians are suffering. In Oxford, on 5 October 1942, a group of people form the Oxford Committee for Famine Relief. Its aim: to relieve the suffering of civilians in Greece, where women and children are starving, and to press for supplies to be allowed through the Allied blockade. The Oxford Committee joins with Famine Relief Committees around the country to lobby British and Allied governments. It is partly successful, and a trickle of food is allowed into Greece before the war ends. But it is only after the liberation of Greece in 1944 that the blockade is finally lifted and the trickle becomes a more adequate supply.

The Oxford Committee raises funds and supplies for the Greek Red Cross to support the victims of conflict. Donations come in through appeals to the public, and through a temporary 'gift shop' where goods are later sold (the forerunner of the now very familiar Oxfam shop).

When peace finally comes, the Oxford Committee finds there is still work to do. More than 30 million refugees are moving across the borders of Europe – with no possessions, homes or future. The Oxford Committee continues to raise money and collect clothing for them. The money pays for food and shelter, and the clothing is shipped to frightened and shattered families in Europe, including the recent enemy – Germany.

In June 1948 the first permanent Oxfam shop (a gift shop and collecting centre) opens in Broad Street, Oxford. There is still an Oxfam shop on the site.

The original Oxford Committee does not disband. It continues to organize relief for refugees from conflict and for victims of natural disasters. In 1965 the telegram name OXFAM is adopted as the registered name of the charity. It expands its activities and its vision and continues on the road to becoming the Oxfam we know today.

Changing times: Oxfam overseas

Oxfam, which started life helping civilian victims and refugees in war-torn Europe, now works in 77 countries and supports over 2,800 long-term development projects. Much of its work is still in areas where conflict makes life almost unsupportable for its innocent victims. A common thread in Oxfam's development is the commitment to humanitarian help for people, irrespective of religious or political boundaries.

Oxfam started as a famine relief organization and is still involved in emergency relief following disasters such as drought, flood or war. But Oxfam is also committed to the wider and more lasting relief of suffering. It works alongside the very poorest people developing ways to break free of sickness, illiteracy, powerlessness and poverty, and arguing against the injustice that causes them.

It helps to challenge the exploitation and injustice that keeps people poor. Local Oxfam staff based around the world keep in regular contact with project partners, giving support and advice, and ensuring that grants are well spent. Many self-help projects are small-scale and only need minimal financial support. About a third of the grants Oxfam makes are for under £3,000, but the impact of these small sums is considerable. After decades of experience Oxfam knows that the projects most likely to succeed are those which engage people in working for their own development.

Oxfam's most public face is its response to disasters and emergencies. The Emergencies Warehouse is a common image on television, with supplies being loaded, often under floodlights, for dispatch to a disaster area. In its early years Oxfam provided shelter, blankets and warm clothes to people displaced by disasters. Now it has a world-wide emergencies service providing water purification, sanitation, medical, housing and other support services, as well as funds for materials and skills available at the site of the disaster. Technology has changed over time but the dedication and commitment is the same.

Here are very brief accounts of just three projects that Oxfam has supported. They show the very wide range of its work and interests, and in this case, focus on projects run by and for women.

In Bangladesh, Saptagram (Seven Villages) began working with women in 1976. It now has a membership of 50,000 women in 700 villages. Rokeya Kabir is the founder of Saptagram. She describes how it works: 'The women form groups which organize awareness building and legal rights classes, as well as adult education and literacy, family planning, health and pure water, and legal aid programmes. Saptagram has overcome important cultural prohibitions; today women move freely in the community, organizing and running training and income-generating projects. They have become involved in traditionally male jobs like brick-making, sinking tubewells, operating power tillers and using weaving machines.'

Oxfam has supported Saptagram since its founding, mainly with grants for salaries and start-up grants for specific projects.

In Zambia, Tiyeseko (We will try) is a women's agricultural project based in the village of Chapita, in the Eastern Province. The group of sixteen women share tasks: 'We work in each other's fields,' says Tisuake Zulu, one of the group members. 'We share the burden and the results of our work.' The group has individual plots of land and a communal field of hybrid maize needing chemical fertilizer. Tiyeseko realized that relying on expensive chemical fertilizers not only caught them in a credit trap (they had to borrow money to buy fertilizer) but it also destroyed the

149

soil. So the group started to grow alternative cash crops like groundnuts, beans and vegetables, and local maize for home consumption. 'The results have been outstanding,' says Tisuake. 'This year I have no hunger in my house.'

Oxfam supported the establishment of Tiyeseko, sponsored the workshop where the members of Tiyeseko developed their new strategy, and funded seeds and a loan fund to enable the group to establish their new and diversified agricultural programme.

In Bolivia, Centro Popular de Salud, Educacion y Produccion, CENPOSEP, is based in San Pedro on the outskirts of Potosi, a city built on the wealth of the silver and tin mines of the Cerro Rico. CENPOSEP is an integrated project involving community health (a health centre, pharmacy and a crèche) and production (a bakery, vegetable gardens and a solar greenhouse). Serapia Colque de Quispe first became involved with CENPOSEP in 1986. 'I wanted to send my three youngest children to the crèche,' she recalls, 'but I had no money to pay the quota. So they said I could work in the bakery and they put me on the rota. Now I join in all the activities, and I'm learning a lot. And, with what I earn in the bakery I can send my older kids to school.' The women of CENPOSEP have learnt many new skills as the project has developed. Serapia tells of learning to read and write: 'When it was my turn to keep the books in the bakery I kept losing count of the bread we'd sold. My husband helped me out, but the others said, "Who's supposed to be working here – you or your husband?" I almost left in tears, I got so discouraged. But in the end I managed to read and write, and now I can keep the books on my own.'

Oxfam supports CENPOSEP with grants, most recently for salaries, education materials, transport, machinery repair and building materials.

'Today women move freely in the community.'
'This year I have no hunger in my house.'
'Now I can keep the books on my own.'
The words of people with whom Oxfam works around the world, describe important advances for individuals and their communities.

Changing times: Oxfam in the UK and Ireland
In 1942 the Oxford Committee was involved in public advocacy – through lobbying, letter-writing and public education, in its campaign to get aid to Greece through the blockade. Since then campaigning and education has been an integral part of Oxfam's work, informing people and governments in the rich world about what can be done to help poorer people in the countries of the South tackle poverty and global injustice.

Oxfam pioneered the charity shop, and for many the term 'Oxfam Shop' *means* charity shop. There are now over 850 Oxfam shops in the UK and Ireland, and shops in Germany and Italy.

The Oxfam catalogue has become a regular source of imaginative gifts, with over 2.5 million copies distributed each year. The catalogue is crammed with craft goods from groups supported by Oxfam's Bridge programme. Bridge provides an outlet for goods produced as part of self-help development projects, backed up by marketing and training support. Other Oxfams have developed the Bridge concept: there are similar projects and mail-order catalogues in the USA, Canada, Australia and Belgium.

Oxfam pioneered fund-raising methods that are now commonplace: sponsored walks and rides; pledged giving; concerts (its 21st birthday rally and concert in 1963 was the first of its kind); charity Christmas cards; covenants; books (Oxfam receives a royalty from every copy of this book sold); national bring-and-buy sales; and many others. Over 60% of Oxfam's funds in the UK and Ireland come from people making donations or a covenanted gift, buying Bridge goods from the catalogue, sending Oxfam cards at Christmas, using Oxfam shops, and taking part in local and national fund-raising events. 79% of the money raised is spent on overseas work and related campaigning and education.

Since 1942 Oxfam has spread across the world, to the USA, to English- and French-speaking Canada, to Australia (where it is called Community Aid Abroad), to Hong Kong, and to Belgium. What started in Oxford is now an international family of independent agencies closely linked to other development organizations throughout the world.

Oxfam: Working for a fairer world

Since its inception Oxfam's support has been given irrespective of race, colour, gender, politics or religion. This support can come in many ways. It may be:

- an improvement in life for the woman who can draw water from a well in her village without having to walk many kilometres,
- providing shelter and support for the refugee, even for a short time,
- two meals a day, instead of one, as a result of improved agricultural methods,
- a landless farmer finally getting title to some land, and with it the freedom to feed his family,
- the relief given by someone who is prepared to listen to your troubles,
- the joy of a mother whose child's life has been saved by oral rehydration,
- the lifting of some oppression through the activity of an unknown friend in a far country, who cared enough to lobby their MP.

Oxfam gives an opportunity for everyone to make this support possible, to make our world a fairer place.

Here are some ways you can help Oxfam work for a fairer world. You could:

- give good quality books, toys, clothes or other things you no longer need to an Oxfam shop,
- save stamps or coins for Oxfam (drop them off at an Oxfam shop),
- organize a social event (coffee morning, jumble sale or bring-and-buy sale) to raise money for Oxfam,
- talk to other people – your friends, your colleagues, the rest of your family – about ways of working for a fairer world, and get yourself and them involved,
- volunteer your time and your skills to work with Oxfam – in a shop, as a campaigner, as a speaker, as a house-to-house collector, as a fundraiser,
- refuse to give up on the world!

To find out more about Oxfam write to us:

in England: OXFAM, Anniversary Information, 274 Banbury Road, Oxford OX2 7DZ

in Ireland: OXFAM, 202 Lower Rathmines Road, Dublin 6

in Northern Ireland: OXFAM, PO Box 70, 52–54 Dublin Road, Belfast, BT2 7HN

in Scotland: OXFAM, Fleming House, 5th Floor, 134 Renfrew Street, Glasgow G3 3T

in Wales: OXFAM, 46–48 Station Road, Llanishen, Cardiff CF4 5LU

in Australia: Community Aid Abroad, 156 George Street, Fitzroy, Victoria 3065

in Belgium: OXFAM Belgique, 39 Rue du Conseil, 1050 Bruxelles

in Canada: OXFAM Canada, 251 Laurier Avenue W, Room 301, Ottawa, Ontario K1P 5J6

in Hong Kong: OXFAM, Ground Floor – 3B, June Garden, 28 Tung Chau Street, Tai Kok Tsui, Kowloon, Hong Kong

in New Zealand: OXFAM New Zealand, Room 101, La Gonda House, 203 Karangahape Road, Auckland 1

in Quebec: OXFAM Quebec, 169 Rue St Paul est, Montreal 127, Quebec H2Y 1G8

in the USA: OXFAM America, 115 Broadway, Boston, Massachusetts 02116

Thank you for buying *Loaves and Wishes*.
You have already contributed to Oxfam's
work as money from each copy sold
supports Oxfam's literacy fund.
We hope you enjoy the book
and that we can count on your support in
the future
WORKING FOR A FAIRER WORLD.

Other Virago books of interest

MARGARET ATWOOD

'An acute and poetic observer of the eternal, universal, rum relations
between women and men'
— *The Times*

*Surfacing, The Edible Woman, Lady Oracle, Dancing Girls, Life Before
Man, Bodily Harm, The Handmaid's Tale, Bluebeard's Egg, Cat's Eye,
Wilderness Tips, Poems 1965–1975, Poems 1976–1986*

SHASHI DESHPANDE

'Refreshingly unselfconscious . . . expressive of the inner world of women
in Indian society . . . The novel's strength lies in its compassion, its
tolerance and understanding of human relationships'
— *The Times Literary Supplement*

Winner of one of India's most prestigious prizes,
the Sahitya Akademi Award

That Long Silence

Also by Shashi Deshpande, *The Great Divide*, forthcoming 1993

ATTIA HOSAIN

'With its beautiful evocation of India, its political insight and
unsentimental understanding of the human heart, *Sunlight on a Broken
Column* is a classic of Muslim life'
— *Time Out*

Sunlight on a Broken Column

Also by Attia Hosain, twelve classic short stories from India, *Phoenix Fled*

MOLLY KEANE

'Take any book by Molly Keane and I guarantee you will be delighted,
warmed and sustained with pleasures . . . She is a born writer'
– *Dirk Bogarde*

*Loving Without Tears, Full House, Conversation Piece, Treasure Hunt,
Taking Chances, Two Days in Aragon, Young Entry, Mad Puppetstown,
The Rising Tide, Devoted Ladies*

SARA MAITLAND

'An outstanding writer'
– *The Times*

Virgin Territory, Daughter of Jerusalem, Three Times Table

CHINATSU NAKAYAMA

'With the delicacy of the Lady Murasaki born again, and the vividness of
high-resolution TV, Chinatsu Nakayama gives the new generation of
adventurous Japanese women their longed-for voice'
– *Clive James*

Behind the Waterfall

ELEAN THOMAS

'Memorable . . . Thomas' Jamaican speech both sings and stings'
– *Observer*

The Last Room